D0900090

MAP OF SITES
OF ROMANESQUE SCULPTURE
ILLUSTRATED IN BOTH VOLUMES.

DURHAM

Bridekirk

Newton-in-Cleveland

Alne
YORK
Bridlington
Kirkburn
Selby
Brayton
Fishlake

LINCOLN

Southwell
Tutbury
Lenton
STAFFORD
Thorpe Arnold
Shernborne
Uffington
Much Wenlock
Coleshill
Wansford
Castor
Fincham
NORWICH
Stottesdon
West
Barton
Ely
Byton
Chaddesley Corbett
Haddon
Seagrave
Eardisley
Castle Frome
Barford
NORTHAMPTON
• 1 ~ Brinsop
• 2 ~ Stretton Sugwas
• 3 ~ Brandwardine
3 Hereford
Hook
Deerhurst
Norton
Kilpeck
GLOUCESTER
Hanborough
OXFORD
Elkstone
Iffley
Gt. Kimble
Moreton Valence
Southrop
Chawley Basset
Stanton Fitzwarren
LONDON
Malmesbury
Barking
Avebury
Amington
READING
Dartford
Rochester
Bobbing
CANTERBURY
Glastonbury
Old Sarum
WINCHESTER
Barfreston
Romsey
Steyning
LEWES
Luppitt
Orchester
Bramber
Alphington
Toller Fratrum
Brighton
Bishop's Teignton
Wareham
St. Marychurch
BODMIN
South Milton

R.L. Pugh

LATER ENGLISH ROMANESQUE SCULPTURE

1140-1210

Jerzy

(GEORGE) ZARNECKI
PH.D., M.A.

NB
463
.Z38

1953
ALEC TIRANTI LTD.
72 CHARLOTTE STREET,
LONDON, W.1

109746

CONTENTS

Made and printed in the United Kingdom

The Beak-head Ornament

The previous volume of this essay brought the history of English sculpture up to about 1140. At this date, after some seventy years of development, English Romanesque sculpture had already reached its maturity. The Anglo-Norman style, which was enriched by the survival of some Anglo-Saxon forms, was by then well established all over the country. It was adopted not only in the big towns and monastic centres, but even in the most remote villages; the restrained and severe architecture, which was characteristic of the earlier Anglo-Norman period, gave way to the more elegant style, in which plastic decoration played a prominent part.

Artistic activity during the long, unhappy period of the Great Anarchy of King Stephen's reign was less affected by political events than might be expected from the accounts of bloodshed, pillage and misery inflicted on the country by both contending parties. Except in the centres which suffered most, churches were built and decorated as before, books illuminated and a variety of objects made in metal and ivory. In fact, this period witnessed great achievements in sculpture.

In contrast to the Anglo-Norman architecture of about 1140, which deliberately abandoned its progressive elements in favour of certain old-fashioned forms that were associated with the " good old days " of English supremacy before 1066, the sculpture of the period was receptive to new ideas from many sources. It is true that the tendency, which was characteristic of architecture, to look back to pre-Conquest times for inspiration, was not entirely absent in sculpture. One cannot, however, speak of English sculpture as a single unit; there were many and sometimes conflicting tendencies in sculpture in different parts of the country and, occasionally, even in one scheme of decoration. Thus in some parts of England, pre-Conquest sculptural traditions lasted longer and expressed themselves in more vigorous forms than in others.

One of the most striking examples of the revival of Anglo-Saxon forms in the twelfth century is found in the enrichment known as the *Beak-head*. It is generally and probably rightly believed that the ultimate origin of this type of decoration was Scandinavian. The immediate source for twelfth century sculptors was, however, Anglo-Saxon beasts' heads, like those found in the tenth century church at Deerhurst, and one discovered in Gloucester and preserved in the local museum. The Deerhurst heads serve as the terminations to an arch label and are enriched by a number of parallel grooves which give a highly decorative effect. The earliest beak-heads known to us, carved about 1130, are those which originally decorated the arches of the cloister at Reading Abbey. Some of them are now preserved at Reading (Museum and the Forbury Gardens), at Shiplake in Oxfordshire and in the Victoria and Albert Museum. They resemble heads of birds with large beaks curving over a roll-moulding of the arch. The character of these heads and their parallel grooves forming a surface-pattern, are so similar to those of the Deerhurst heads that it seems very probable that the Reading beak-heads are derived from an Anglo-Saxon form put, however, to a new architectural use. The actual application of the beak-heads to the decoration of arches was consistent with, and a further development of the Anglo-Norman method of decorating arches with the chevron ornament, or even with isolated triangles superimposed on the roll-mouldings as at Romsey Abbey. It was a logical development in keeping with the love of exuberant decoration, to apply sculpture of some kind to these triangles. The sculptor who first enriched an arch with heads modelled on an Anglo-Saxon prototype obviously expressed the mood of the age very well. From about 1130 to 1180 this type of decoration became not only the fashion in English architecture, but was also adopted in Normandy and even further afield.

It has been said of this decoration that its absence from

cathedrals and larger monastic buildings implies that even in the twelfth century it was regarded as somewhat barbaric. The almost savage character of some of the beak-heads cannot be denied, but an equal amount, if not more, are grotesque or even humorous. Moreover, a careful search reveals that there were originally beak-heads in such important churches as Westminster Abbey, Christ Church at Oxford, Old Sarum Cathedral, Dorchester Abbey, Bridlington Priory, and Reading Abbey, in addition to the well-known examples still in their original position at Lincoln Cathedral. This list is therefore sufficient to suggest that, on the contrary, some of the most important churches were enriched by this type of decoration.

A study of the geographical distribution of the beak-head ornament shows that there were two regions where it was particularly popular, namely Oxfordshire and Yorkshire. Those in Oxfordshire seem to have been influenced by Reading and it was also through the cell of Reading Abbey at Leominster that this decoration was probably introduced into Herefordshire. From Oxfordshire and the neighbouring counties the beak-head ornament spread further north to Southwell and Lincoln. Yorkshire adopted this motive about 1160 and it was in that region that it enjoyed its greatest popularity and that an amazing number of variations were evolved. In the south-east of the country, the beak-head ornament is comparatively rare.

Figs. 10, 11, 104

Fig. 19

Fig. 49

Figs. 75, 83

At Reading, the beak-heads were already being used in alternation with grotesque heads. Soon, in addition to the actual birds' heads, heads of other animals and even human heads were used to decorate the mouldings of arches. From the arches this decoration spread to the shafts; Old Sarum, Lincoln and Barford (1140—50) are probably the earliest examples of this method. At Barford and Tutbury there are as many as two shafts on either side of the doorway decorated in this manner. In its final stage of development, the beak-head ornament was applied not only to the arches of doorways and shafts, but also to the nave arcades, the

Figs. 43, 11, 49

Fig. 103

chancel arches and occasionally even to capitals, windows and ribs of vaulting.

Figure sculpture at the end of the first half of the twelfth century varied considerably in character and quality. On the whole, in out of the way places the decorative style of the earlier part of the twelfth century was retained, though with some modifications. In contrast, however, to the earlier emphasis on foliage and animal motives, there was at that time an increasing interest in the human figure. A capital at *Fig.* 1 Westminster Abbey, which dates from about 1140, shows a new interest in careful modelling, while the proportions of the human body are more balanced, and its movements more natural. In the scene of the *Judgment of Solomon*, the means of expression are still naive, but the simplicity and sincerity of this work resulted in a highly successful and moving composition.

Medieval artists seldom carved human figures in the nude. Drapery was therefore the principal means of expressing the shape and movement of the body. Sometimes the drapery formed a pattern that covered and masked the body instead *Figs.* 2, 4 of modelling it. In very many cases when a sculptor worked with the help of a pattern book, as undoubtedly he often did, the influence of drawing technique on his work is clearly *Fig.* 7 visible.

Unfortunately, not a single English pattern-book from the twelfth century survives. They must have been widely used because identical patterns are often found in the decoration of two or more buildings and, even if it is assumed that in all these cases the similarity was due to a common authorship, the agreement of complicated patterns is often too close to have been based only on the memory of an artist. Furthermore, two such similar works sometimes show differences of treatment, which excludes the possibility of their being carved by the same sculptor.

8

The Herefordshire School

Perhaps the most striking case of the use of pattern-books in the whole history of English Romanesque sculpture, is supplied by a group of monuments in Herefordshire and the neighbouring counties.

This remarkable school came into being about 1140, at the height of the Civil War and, surprisingly, in one of its centres. It was in 1138 that Hereford, garrisoned by the supporters of Matilda, was besieged by King Stephen. Before the city surrendered, it was severely damaged by fire. Miles of Gloucester, later Earl of Hereford, retook the city for Matilda the following year.

It was at exactly this time that Shobdon Church was erected, and it was in this building that the sculpture of the " Herefordshire School " was initiated. A remarkable document, preserved in the University Library at Chicago, tells us the circumstances of the foundation of this church. It was founded by Oliver de Merlimond, chief steward of Hugh de Mortimer, Lord of Wigmore. When the building was begun, the document tells us, Oliver went on a pilgrimage to Santiago de Compostela in Spain, to pay homage to the relics of St. James. He made the journey by way of France and not by sea, as we are told that on his way back he was the guest of the canons of Saint-Victor in Paris. When the church was finished it was dedicated by Robert de Bethune, Bishop of Hereford. The Abbot of Saint-Victor was then asked to send some of his canons to Shobdon. Their stay in England was at first very unhappy. Feudal disturbances and violence caused them great hardship and they suffered particularly from a quarrel between Hugh de Mortimer and Oliver de Merlimond, which ended with Hugh's seizure of Shobdon. Eventually the canons moved to Wigmore where they founded an abbey.

Shobdon Church was pulled down in the eighteenth

century and its two doorways with their, once magnificent, tympana and the chancel arch, were re-erected in Shobdon Park as a triumphal arch, which is now decaying from exposure. From the events mentioned in the foundation document, it is possible to fix the date of the building of Shobdon to between 1131 and 1143, of which the last five years seem to be the most likely date. It must have been a magnificent, though comparatively small, building. Its sculpture astonishes us with its mixture of styles and motives. Some of them go back to pre-Conquest times and can be paralleled by the decoration of Anglo-Saxon crosses. There are also links with Scandinavian art, while some motives appear to have been borrowed from Reading and others from Western France. For a student of English medieval sculpture, Shobdon is an exciting and puzzling subject of stylistic analysis. The deplorable condition of this monument deprives it, however, of much of its original beauty and, for this reason, it is more convenient to turn to other examples of the Herefordshire School in order to examine its characteristics.

The best preserved church of the school is at Kilpeck. This church has a wealth of sculpture lavished on its doorway, chancel arch, corbels and windows. One can see that at least three different hands were at work on its decoration, although the differences between individual styles are not great. At Shobdon these differences are much more marked, as if the sculptors, each with his individual style, were here assembled for the first time to work as a team.

Figs. 19, 20, 22—24
Almost all the merits and defects of the school can be assessed on examining the doorway at Kilpeck, which has been extraordinarily well preserved, thanks to a wooden porch which protected it for centuries until it was unwisely removed just over a hundred years ago. The sculpture of this doorway is most original, both in its motives and its application. The main arch is carved with beak-heads, monsters and an angel, which is placed at the apex. *Fig.* 22 The label has a chain motive, each ring containing a bird or a monster and one the Fishes

10

of the Zodiac. The jambs of the doorway are covered with thick bodies of twisting snakes, and one of the shafts with figures of warriors intertwining with foliage, while the other *Fig.* 20 is carved with foliage and a pair of doves at the base. The capitals are decorated with animals and a grotesque head. On the tympanum a vine-scroll forms a symmetrical design. The star pattern on the abaci, and the chevron on the inner order of the arch and the lintel are the only conventional Anglo-Norman motives used in the decoration of this doorway. The beak-heads show a great variety of design. Great technical skill, amazing vitality of character and inventiveness of motive are the chief merits of this work. There is, however, a certain over-exuberance of decoration that spreads from one architectural member to another, obscuring their division; for example the shafts and the jambs are hardly distinguishable from each other. Again, the common decoration obscures the division between the capitals and the jambs; there is no clear division between the tympanum and the lintel. Finally, the label with its chain-motive is far too heavy for the slender supports of the arch. This lack of clarity and overloading with decoration springs, quite obviously, from the tremendous vitality of the sculptors who, one almost feels, having once begun their work, could hardly restrain themselves.

The decoration of the exterior of the church includes the richly carved west window and a magnificent series of corbels carved in the form of grotesque heads and animals. Projecting *Fig.* 29 from the angles of the nave and from the centre of the west front are large heads of dragons, carved as openwork and *Fig.* 26 reminiscent of Scandinavian art. Similar heads decorate the gables of twelfth century wooden churches in Norway, and in minor arts such heads were already in use in the eleventh century, if not earlier. A Viking comb found in London and preserved in the Guildhall Museum is enriched with a head, *Fig.* 27 which bears a striking resemblance to the Kilpeck corbels and perhaps indicates that this motive was introduced into England by the Vikings in the eleventh century.

The decoration of the chancel arch at Kilpeck consists of the usual Anglo-Norman geometrical enrichment of the arch but the shafts have a motive which was, until then, totally unknown in England. Each shaft is decorated with *Fig. 21* the figures of three apostles, one above the other. It is well known that column-figures were used on a big scale in such churches as Saint-Denis and Chartres, which were more or less contemporary with Kilpeck. The origin of the Kilpeck shafts, however, has to be sought not in the monumental sculpture of the Ile-de-France where single over life-size figures were attached to shafts, but in buildings where the idea of column-figures was less developed and where several smaller figures were placed one above the other. Our attention must inevitably turn to the document describing the foundation of Shobdon and the journey of its founder to Santiago de Compostela. It is there, at Compostela, in the famous early twelfth century doorway, the *Puerta de las Platerias*, that we find marble shafts, each carved with three pairs of figures one above the other.

The existence of such a distant relationship may seem at first hardly credible, but the careful analysis of other works of the Herefordshire School reveals a number of motives derived from monuments along the pilgrimage route from Paris to Compostela. In particular, the decoration of the churches of the Poitou and Charente districts of Western France shows strong links with Herefordshire. Thus, it becomes clear that the reference to the journey of Oliver de Merlimond to Compostela is of great significance, and we must assume that one of the sculptors employed by him at Shobdon was included in his retinue. While on the journey he obviously made sketches of a number of decorative schemes in France and Spain, which he later used at Shobdon, Kilpeck and other places.

A striking confirmation of this theory is found in two works *Fig. 31* of the Herefordshire School, namely the tympana at Brinsop and Stretton Sugwas, about two miles apart from each other. The first represents St. George on horseback, thrusting

12

his spear into the dragon, whose snake-like body is trampled on by the horse. St. George is represented as a contemporary knight with hawks. The tympanum at Stretton Sugwas *Fig.* 32 shows Samson struggling with the lion. He sits astride the beast and forces open its jaws.

One of the churches visited by the pilgrims going from Paris to Compostela was that at Parthenay-le-Vieux (Deux-Sèvres) built about 1120. On its west front there are two *Fig.* 33 tympana. The one to the north of the central doorway represents a rider with a hawk trampling on the body of an enemy. There are many similar sculptures with riders in Western France and there is reason to believe that they were derived from the equestrian statue of Marcus Aurelius, then in the Lateran, which had, in the Middle Ages, been mistakenly believed to represent Constantine the Great. The Brinsop St. George, through its intermediate sources in Western France, is ultimately derived from that ancient Roman prototype. If we are still not convinced about the relationship of the St. George at Brinsop and the Constantine at Parthenay-le-Vieux, details common to both, such as the cloak which flows out behind each rider, should remove any doubts. In both cases the horses ride from left to right. The Herefordshire sculptor saw the French tympanum when it was still a new work and its splendour was, no doubt, heightened by the rich colours with which it was painted. He made a sketch of the tympanum in his pattern-book, as well as of the other tympanum on the south side of the west front. This represents Samson and the lion and although it is very damaged, one can still see that at Stretton Sugwas the attitudes of the struggling figures facing the north were copied from this French model. The Herefordshire sculptor had no opportunity of using his sketches in the decoration of one church, so he used each drawing for a separate building.

In addition to the churches already mentioned, the Herefordshire School includes the decoration of Leominster Priory and Rowlestone. The first of these was a cell of

Reading Abbey and, although its sculptures date from about 1150 and are thus not by any means the earliest in the development of the school, they show an unmistakable link with Reading, which was decorated some twenty years earlier. The cloister at Leominster, which is no longer in existence was carved earlier than the west front. It was probably the main example of the Reading style in Herefordshire, and it was from here, one can assume, that many elements characteristic of Reading were transmitted to Herefordshire.

The decoration of Rowlestone exhibits such a remarkable uniformity of style that this must have been the work of one sculptor. The quality of this decoration does not achieve the usual high level which is characteristic of the Herefordshire School. The almost mechanical repetition of motives from a pattern-book resulted here in a somewhat lifeless work, although technically it is still very skilful.

Single tympana at Fownhope, Hereford, and Ruardean in Gloucestershire and a corbel at Orleton are today the only signs of the activities of the Herefordshire School in these places. At Rock in Worcestershire, it is possible to recognise the work of one of the Herefordshire sculptors in the decoration of the chancel arch. His works are easily distinguishable at Shobdon, Kilpeck and elsewhere, as his style is more restrained than that of the other sculptors of the school. His early work, the tympanum at Aston, was undoubtedly executed before he was called to work at Shobdon. His style at a later date can be studied on the font at Stottesdon Fig. 34 in Shropshire, which has as its principal decoration a chain-Fig. 19 motive similar to that on the Kilpeck doorway.

The Stottesdon font is not the only one that bears the style of the Herefordshire School. There are several others. The Fig. 25 font at Eardisley is carved with fighting warriors and the *Harrowing of Hell*. This last subject was also employed on a tympanum at Shobdon. At Castle Frome, the sculpture of the font is confined to religious subjects only: the symbols Fig. 30 of the Evangelists and the *Baptism of Christ*. This last scene is full of naive charm. The font rests on a base carved with

14

three crouching figures carved in the round in the style of *Fig.* 28 the best Kilpeck corbels. The beautifully shaped font at *Fig.* 29 Chaddesley Corbett in Worcestershire is decorated with *Fig.* 35 inter-twining dragons and interlacing bands. Other fonts of the school are found at Shobdon and Orleton.

The significance of the Herefordshire School is great. It is in the works of this group of sculptors that we can detect for the first time since the Norman Conquest, the strong influence of Continental centres on English sculpture. The influence of Spanish sculpture is rather unexpected and so is that of Western France long before the accession of Henry II, under whose rule the Angevin provinces were united with England.

In comparison with an earlier school of English sculpture which blossomed in Southern England between 1120 and 1140, the Herefordshire School shows an important change in patronage. The greatest works of the Southern School are found in the monastic houses and they show a close similarity of style with contemporary illuminations made in those monastic centres. The works of the Herefordshire School, on the other hand, were executed for lay patrons. This is reflected in the smaller size of the churches, the greater stress on their elaborate decorations and the choice of subjects, which include many taken from contemporary life such as fighting warriors or animals and birds used in hunting.

III

First Italian Influences.   The Tournai Imports

From about 1140, contact between English and Continental sculpture became increasingly frequent, although it is doubtful whether this was due to the journeys of artists, as in the case of the sculptor of the Herefordshire School. More probably the patron, who was particularly impressed by a foreign decorative scheme, acted as a transmitting agent. In many cases this is the only plausible explanation of the appearance in England of a foreign motive executed in the local style.

Let us take as an example the caryatids from the chapter house of Durham Cathedral, built between 1133 and 1140. *Figs. 36—37* These figures, which happily survived the destruction of the chapter house in the eighteenth century, are about half life-size and they support heavy capitals, decorated in a style closely connected with that of the north doorway of the cathedral, dating from about 1130. Large-scale figures carrying a weight on their shoulders were an antique motive, revived in Northern Italy early in the twelfth century and from there transmitted to other countries.

If the Durham caryatids in their general structure can be compared to many Italian figures of the first three decades of the twelfth century, for instance to the figures of the cathedral at Piacenza, their hard geometrical folds are, however, English in character. These works of great power and beauty testify that English sculptors were capable of successfully adopting foreign models to their particular mode of expression. It is very illuminating to follow the evolution in the treatment of figures and folds on the seals of dignity of the Bishops of Durham, for these can be dated fairly accurately. We thus find that the seal of Bishop Geoffrey Rufus, who built the chapter house, is very similar to some of the Durham caryatids, particularly to one representing a standing bishop or some other ecclesiastic. It has the same shape of vestments on which folds are marked by mere incised lines, as on the standing figure of the bishop on the seal. The first seal of Bishop William of St. Barbe (1143—1152) is also of a similar type, but in the second seal not only are the vestments differently shaped, but the treatment of folds is more plastic and accentuated. All successive seals carry this development a step further. As can be expected, the only close analogy with the stone caryatids is to be found in the seal of the bishop who built the chapter house. We need no better confirmation of their date.

Beside the French and Italian influences on English sculpture of this period, yet another foreign artistic penetration was taking place. This came from Flanders and took a more direct form through the importation of various objects from the Tournai region. Tournai marble, like the alabaster of Nottinghamshire in a later period, gave birth to a flourishing trade in carved objects such as fonts, tombs, capitals, and columns. These were transported by sea and rivers and are found all over Northern Europe.

The Tournai fonts must have been highly thought of in England at the time, as we find them not only in provincial churches but in such important buildings as Lincoln and Winchester Cathedrals. The Winchester font is perhaps the *Figs.* 38—39 best of those that survive in England, but even this has all the faults of a mass-produced work, particularly in its lifeless narrative and stereotyped figures. More attractive are those carvings on the Tournai fonts which have a purely decorative and not narrative function. These were frequently imitated in England and perhaps the most striking example of such an English-made font, based on the Tournai style, is a late twelfth century font at Newenden in Kent.

Fonts were not the only carved objects exported from Tournai to England. A marble capital from Old Sarum, preserved in the Museum at Salisbury, is of Flemish workman- *Fig.* 40 ship. We know from an old drawing that an identical capital once existed at Glastonbury. We do not know the material from which it was made, but there are still a few fragments of marble capitals in the Abbey Museum at Glastonbury, all exhibiting a style very close to that of the Old Sarum capital. Thus it seems certain that all these capitals were brought to England ready-made from Flanders and used in places widely separated. Some marble capitals from the Cluniac Priory of St. Pancras at Lewes, now in the local museum, are also of Flemish workmanship, but they are later in date and different in style.

Some tomb-slabs were also brought from Tournai, but they show a greater variety of design than the fonts. However, like the fonts, they were mass-produced and then exported for sale and thus, to be acceptable to any future buyer, the designs were either symbolical or ornamental, sometimes both, but always avoiding the representation of the deceased person, whose status and sex could not be foreseen. For instance a tomb-slab at Bridlington Priory in Yorkshire is carved with purely decorative motives, and one at Ely Cathedral has St. Michael the Archangel carrying the soul *Fig.* 41 of the dead. In both cases the slabs could have been used for the tomb of any person. Incidentally, the treatment of the Archangel's dress on the Ely slab is so reminiscent of the Winchester font, that both probably came from the same workshop. The tomb of Gundrada at Lewes is sometimes considered to be a Tournai product but this is far from certain. The long inscription on the slab could have been added in England, but the foliage decoration has some English characteristics and in this case, therefore, it is more likely that the marble was brought from Tournai but the work executed at Lewes.

In spite of all these artistic intrusions from abroad, a great deal of mid-twelfth century sculpture in England remained little affected by foreign influences. Earlier traditions, especially those of the Southern School, enriched by new motives, spread far beyond the original boundaries of this school. A particularly splendid mid-century example is St. *Figs.* 14—17 Peter's Church at Northampton. A series of capitals there combines foliage and animal decoration with an occasional

18

human figure. A tomb-slab in this church was carved by the Fig. 18
same group of sculptors. It is covered by a profusion of
purely decorative motives and, like the sculpture of the
Southern School, shows a great indebtedness to manuscript
illuminations. The much restored chancel arch of St. Chad's
in Stafford shows a style connected with Northampton.

It was typical of carvers' workshops at this time, that the
scope of their activities became much wider than in the
earlier part of the century. The work of the Southern
School, for instance, was limited to the decoration of churches
and only one font, that at Reading, can be safely attributed
to this school. In the Herefordshire School, on the other
hand, the decoration of the church fittings was clearly also
the rule. From the workshop which was responsible for the
decoration of St. Peter's at Northampton, came the tomb-slab
in that church, as well as fonts at Harpole and Mears Ashby.

However, only works of a provincial character in this period
show a complete lack of contact with artistic developments
abroad. The sculpture of the big centres invariably assimilated
the achievements of various foreign centres. The process was
reciprocal however, and English sculpture in turn supplied
models to Normandy and thence to other regions.

IV

Lincoln

One of the most important decorative schemes undertaken in England in the twelfth century was the west front of Lincoln Cathedral. In this scheme English and foreign elements mix freely and the results achieved are most happy. The importance of Lincoln compels us to examine its decoration in some detail.

The original Anglo-Norman structure of the cathedral was completed at the end of the eleventh century but after a fire in 1141, the nave and the west front were altered by Bishop Alexander (1123—1148). Bishop Alexander was known for his extravagant and luxurious tastes, which earned him the name of Alexander the Magnificent. He was a nephew of Roger, the powerful Bishop of Salisbury, to whose influence he owed his career. He was first made Archdeacon of Sarum, a fact which was perhaps not without significance when some details of his scheme of reconstruction at Lincoln are examined. He paid two visits to Italy in 1125 and 1145 and several to France. We can thus presume that he was well aware of the artistic achievements in those countries, and this is confirmed by an examination of the west front of Lincoln.

Although damaged by fire, this west front remained fundamentally a late eleventh century structure with three enormous recessed arches. Bishop Alexander's reconstruction consisted mainly of furnishing these arches with richly decorated doorways and building above them a blind arcade, surmounted by a gable. Just above the doorways, across the whole width of the building a carved frieze was inserted.

The date of the sculptures of the west front of Lincoln has been disputed for more than a hundred years, but the most generally accepted view is that the doorways are part of Bishop Alexander's work and were thus carved between 1141 and 1148, while the frieze marks the completion of the reconstruction, some years after his death.

The Italian inspiration of the Lincoln frieze is obvious. No other church but Modena has a frieze of a similar type and with a similar choice of subjects. When Bishop Alexander made his journeys to Rome, he probably took the usual route, the Via Emilia, which led him through Modena, where he must have been struck by Guglielmo's highly individual work. It is not the style of Guglielmo's sculptures, however, that is reflected at Lincoln, but only the architectural application of the sculptures and their iconographical programme that were imitated here. The closest stylistic analogies for both the figures of the frieze and some of the shafts of the Lincoln doorways are to be found not in Italy, but in France. The church which supplies these analogies is no less important a building than the Cathedral of Saint-Denis.

However surprising this statement may sound at first, there can be no doubt about it. The dates fit admirably. The west front of Saint-Denis was built between 1137 and 1140, that is to say, a year before the fire damaged Lincoln Cathedral. Abbot Suger's artistic activities must have been much discussed and envied by many men and Bishop Alexander, with his ambitions and tastes, was probably one of them. His abilities and resources can hardly be compared to those of Suger's. He did not gather artists from all over Europe for the rebuilding of Lincoln and he obviously did not take such interest in every detail of the work. In fact there is a fundamental difference between Suger's and Alexander's rebuilding. The first wanted to build and for this reason he had to find an excuse to replace the ancient and venerated church by one of his own creation. His west front was begun from the very foundations. Alexander had always shown greater interest in building castles than churches, and his work at Lincoln was forced on him by the accidental fire. He retained the old fabric, made it safe by roofing the nave with a stone vault and altered only the upper parts of the west front. He showed, however, his taste for lavish display by inserting the new doorways and the frieze above them.

The three doorways at Lincoln contain a number of decorative motives that were current in England at that time, especially the chevron and the beak-head ornaments. *Fig.* 54 The beak-heads are applied to one arch of each doorway and *Figs.* 49, 55, on the central doorway, even to the shafts of the inner order. A similar decoration existed at Old Sarum, as is shown by *Figs.* 43, 44, some fragments preserved in Salisbury Museum. The treatment of these beak-heads in both places is so similar that they could have been carved by the same workshop. In view of the family connections between Bishop Alexander and Bishop Roger, and of Alexander's earlier office at Sarum, such a possibility sounds reasonable. Roger died in 1139 and when, two years later, Alexander began the rebuilding of Lincoln, he could have procured the services of his uncle's masons. However, this may account for one motif only, which had previously been used at Sarum. Much more startling is the connection between Lincoln and Saint-Denis.

Unfortunately both Saint-Denis and Lincoln suffered from drastic restoration in the nineteenth century but enough original work remains in both places to show their close relationship. The extensive use of shafts with diaper patterns containing geometrical and foliage motives of similar character, is found both at Saint-Denis and Lincoln. So are the shafts of spiral form, decorated with diamond enrichments. What is, however, most striking is the use of shafts, six at Saint-Denis and four at Lincoln, which are richly covered with the so-called inhabited scrolls, that is to say foliage containing climbing figures, birds and beasts. Many *Figs.* 52, 53, of these are so similar in general treatment, pose, design and their relation to the foliage, that their close connection can *Fig.* 50 hardly be doubted. Moreover, some of the capitals at Lincoln are of the acanthus type, the later version of which reappeared at Canterbury twenty years later under the influence of William of Sens. Even by French standards, the Lincoln capitals are very early examples of that proto-Gothic type, *Fig.* 51 which appears in a very similar form at Saint-Denis. There are also a number of small details common to both places,

22

which make their relationship even closer. The striking similarity of some of the neckings, the use of false abaci, so rare in both countries, yet used on some of the capitals in both places, and the plain bands on most of the shafts at their ends, are only some of them.

As it has been pointed out, the doorways at Lincoln have many typically English characteristics and it is only fair to say that they dominate the motives derived from Saint-Denis. The chevron, the embattled pattern, the beak-heads, the label heads and the scalloped capitals so obscure the foreign-inspired elements that these last escaped the notice of even such an authority as Viollet-le-Duc when he paid a visit to Lincoln nearly a hundred years ago.

Fig. 47

The peculiar thing about the Lincoln doorways is that they show a detailed knowledge of the west front of Saint-Denis without, however, copying its structure and composition. The Lincoln doorways had no tympana, no figure-carved voussoirs and, above all, no figure-columns that formed an essential part of Suger's work. The knowledge of Saint-Denis is too " professional " to have been conveyed to the English sculptors by Bishop Alexander himself. One is very much tempted, even compelled, to attribute that knowledge to a sculptor who actually worked at Saint-Denis and who, when the decoration there was finished in 1140, accepted the offer of Bishop Alexander to come to Lincoln.

The great American scholar, Arthur Kingsley Porter, drew attention to the essentially Italian character of the decoration of Saint-Denis and he pointed out how many of its elements are based on the works of Guglielmo. From Suger's account we know that he gathered artists from all over Europe for his great undertaking. It is thus very likely that one or more of the sculptors were summoned from Lombardy. Perhaps one of the Lincoln sculptors was an Italian, who worked for Suger at Saint-Denis. It is generally accepted that the Lincoln frieze is an imitation of Modena's famous frieze by Guglielmo. There is no such frieze at Saint-Denis, yet the style of some of the scenes of the Lincoln frieze are strikingly similar to the figure-style of Saint-Denis. The only explanation of this phenomenon is their common execution by a sculptor trained in Lombardy.

The Lincoln frieze was disturbed by the subsequent re-setting of at least one of the reliefs; some others are preserved as fragments and a few are missing. Let us briefly examine the frieze. Its subjects form two groups; the Old Testament scenes are placed to the south of the main doorway, those of the New Testament to the north. The Old Testament cycle, as it is preserved today, consists of the following scenes: *Fig.* 57 the *Expulsion from Paradise, Cain and Abel,* the *Birth of Enoch* and below, on the same panel, *Lamech killing Cain, Daniel in the Lions' Den* and several incidents from the story of the Deluge, *Fig.* 60 such as *God speaking to Noah, Noah building the Ark, Noah in the Fig.* 59 *Ark, the Deluge* and *Noah leaving the Ark.* Stylistically, the Old Testament reliefs are uniform and probably the work of a single sculptor, whom it is tempting to call the Italian Master. It is enough to compare the faces, the treatment of the folds and the proportions and gestures of the figures to those of the Saint-Denis reliefs, which have been spared by the *Figs.* 56, restorers, to see how remarkably close they are in style. 58 Often a small detail common in two related works of art is more revealing than a general similarity. In the case of the doorways, we have seen that there are many such details. In the figure-sculpture of Lincoln and Saint-Denis, one can also point to at least two such analogies. One is the use of foliage borders. The small panels with the Signs of the *Fig.* 56 Zodiac and the Labours of the Months at Saint-Denis are framed by elaborate borders of a similar character to those which are employed in three Old Testament reliefs at *Fig.* 57 Lincoln, where, however, they are used not as proper frames but along one side of the relief only. Much more important and indeed revealing, is a detail that is most unusual yet which appears in many Old Testament figures at Lincoln and in almost all the figures at Saint-Denis. This detail shows the front and back hem of the garments in a continuous line as though it were being seen from below. It is sufficient

24

to compare a figure supporting the column of the north doorway at Saint- Denis with the figures on almost any Old Testament relief at Lincoln to realise the identical use of this device. *Fig.* 56 *Figs.* 57, 60

The original sequence of the Old Testament scenes at Lincoln was from the central doorway to the south. The New Testament scenes also begin in the centre of the west front and develop to the north. Of the three reliefs adjoining the central doorway, only a small fragment of one survives. The first complete relief is that of *Dives and Lazarus*. The story *Fig.* 61 is continued in the next relief with the *Death of Lazarus*, whose soul is being taken by angels to Heaven while Dives and his companions are being pushed by a devil into the open mouth of Hell. The next relief represents *Abraham carrying the Souls of the Righteous*. Further to the north is a group of figures, some seated and others standing, includ- *Fig.* 62 ing a bishop, perhaps meant to be St. James. The group consists of six figures, and it is reasonable to suppose that there was a similar group of six figures on the opposite side of the doorway and that they represented the apostles witnessing the *Last Judgment*, which was probably placed over the doorway. This section of the frieze was, however, removed when a large Gothic window was inserted. The fragments of *Christ in Majesty*, now kept inside the cathedral, could have belonged to that part of the composition. The remaining section of the frieze is carved with the scene of the *Harrowing of Hell* and the much restored *Torments of the Damned*. *Fig.* 63 The reliefs above the central doorway were replaced in the fourteenth century by figures of kings. This is a grave loss as it was the most important section of the whole frieze.

Most of the New Testament reliefs show a considerable change in style in comparison with those of the Old Testament The *Apostles* and the *Torments of the Damned* especially are carved in a higher relief than the rest of the panels, and the treatment of the strained draperies of the *Apostles* differs greatly from those of the other figures.

If the reliefs of the Old Testament are stylistically uniform and, as I suggested, the work of a single sculptor, those of the New Testament are by at least two, if not three men. I do not believe that the variety of styles means, in this case, any great difference in the date of execution. Most of the work of reconstruction must have been done in Alexander's lifetime, that is to say before 1148, as we have a trustworthy account by Henry of Huntingdon, who wrote his *Historia Anglorum* at that time. He writes that, after Alexander's return from Rome in 1146, the restoration made necessary by the fire was completed and the church was " more beautiful than before and second to none in the realm." Surely Henry of Huntingdon would not have used this phrase, even if it was a deliberate exaggeration, on account of the new vault of the nave alone. He must have seen or heard about the decoration of the west front. The misleading impression of the date of some of the New Testament reliefs is caused by nineteenth century restoration. One of the panels of the *Torment of the Damned*, for instance, is completely replaced by a new work imitating a style of about 1200. The original reliefs are, however, carved in a style that is quite possible for the middle of the twelfth century. For instance, the figures of the apostles are stylistically foreshadowed by a relief at Rouse Lench in Worcestershire. This interesting relief is related to the Ely tympanum of about 1140 * but is executed in a more plastic style and uses strained folds to cover the limbs. A later development of the same style will be seen at Malmesbury. The lively scenes of the *Torments of the Damned* can also be seen to have good analogies in contemporary English art. A large-scale relief preserved in the Bury St. Edmunds Museum representing a similar subject, although very damaged, still shows a remarkable resemblance to the Lincoln scenes. Moreover, this relief

---

* See Author's *English Romanesque Sculpture, 1066-1140*, Fig. 77. In subsequent quotations this book will be referred to as " Vol. I."

carved on two sides of a rectangular block, seems to have been part of a frieze and came no doubt from the west front of the Abbey, built by Abbot Anselm, who died in 1148.

The fragments of the reliefs kept inside the cathedral at Lincoln are commonly thought to have been part of a single composition, that of *Christ in Majesty*. However, they must have formed two separate reliefs, because on one fragment Christ is represented with the upper part of the mandorla ending in rich foliage, while the other fragment retains two symbols of the Evangelist and a standing figure of an apostle facing a mandorla which is treated with jewel-like enrichment. Thus it is impossible for the two fragments to have belonged to one composition. One Majesty could not have been enclosed by two mandorlas. The first fragment can safely be dated to the middle of the twelfth century. Its foliage has a " dotted " leaf, made popular by manuscripts such as the Bury St. Edmunds Bible now at Corpus Christi College, Cambridge (MS. 2), which was finished before 1148.

The other relief, that of an Apostle, is of a much finer quality and has often been compared to Toulousian sculpture. It seems, however, that the column-figures at Saint-Denis, known to us from Montfaucon's drawings, are the most obvious prototypes for this relief. The masterly modelling of the folds, the crossed legs, the forshortened feet and above all, the treatment of the head, are directly derived from Saint-Denis, obviously through the Italian Master. Moreover, the jewel-like mandorla is also of the same character as the ornament of the Saint-Denis doorways.

The importance of the Lincoln sculptures is self-evident. Here for the first time in English Romanesque sculpture, a truly monumental scheme of decoration was carried out, based on the best foreign models. Whether the suggestion of the actual collaboration of a foreign sculptor with an English workshop be accepted or not, the link established at Lincoln with the Ile-de-France seems beyond any reasonable doubt. This episode in the history of English Romanesque sculpture was perhaps not as isolated as it seems to us today.

Too many twelfth century buildings have perished in the course of centuries to make our study satisfactory on such points as this.

V

Byzantine Influences

Such Italian influence as can be found, for example, in Lincoln, is very much modified by French elements. In some cases, the Italian influence is more direct. For instance, a recently discovered figure of an angel at Bury St. Edmunds is derived from such sculpture as the jamb figures at Ferrara, Nicolo's work of about 1135. In this connection it is worth recalling that Anselm, who was Abbot of Bury from 1121 to 1148, was an Italian. He was formerly Abbot of SS. Alexius and Sabas, a Basilian monastery in Rome and he was undoubtedly very influential in introducing Italian artistic forms to England. He must also have been well acquainted with Byzantine art, as his monastery was founded under the patronage of the Greek centres in Southern Italy. Professor F. Wormald has pointed out that Byzantine elements, which are so strong in the Bury Bible, a manuscript *Fig.* 68 illuminated by Master Hugo during the abbacy of Anselm, were probably due to Anselm's influence.

Of course Anselm was not, by any means, the only person in England at that time who knew Byzantine art. The Crusades brought the Eastern Mediterranean nearer to Western Europe. The Norman conquest of Sicily caused an extraordinary fusion of Byzantine, Islamic and Western art in Southern Italy. The resulting style spread from there to other countries. Finally, the strong and direct influence of Byzantine art on Germany was transmitted from there westwards. The frequent political missions, inter-marriages, exchange of gifts and commerce encouraged the spread of artistic styles.

The relief of the *Virgin and Child* in York Minster, a work *Fig.* 64 of great artistic importance, is an example of the Byzantine influence on English sculpture. The date of this masterpiece has been greatly disputed and it has been suggested by some scholars that it is a product of the Anglo-Saxon period, while others maintain that it is Romanesque. The most eloquent amongst those who supported the Anglo-Saxon date was the late Sir Alfred Clapham, who did so on purely epigraphic grounds. The critics of his method question, however, the accuracy of his arguments, pointing out that the peculiarities of some of the letters of the inscription over the sculpture are not uncommon on English coins and seals of the twelfth century and are by no means confined only to pre-Conquest times, as the great scholar believed.

However, it is generally agreed that the York Virgin is based on a Byzantine model. Of all the Byzantine analogies, which can be suggested for the York Virgin, by far the closest is one that is not of pure Byzantine origin but is an English copy of a Byzantine model, namely the Virgin in the Winchester Psalter, now in the British Museum (Cotton MS. Nero C.IV). Professor O. Demus, an authority on Byzantine art, in his book on *The Mosaics of Norman Sicily*, suggested that the Virgin in the Winchester Psalter is an English copy of a Sicilian prototype.

The undoubted stylistic relationship between the York Virgin and the Virgin in the Winchester Psalter indicates that their models came from the same source which, as Professor Demus pointed out in the case of the Psalter, was the Byzantine art of Sicily. Such an explanation is historically more than probable. It should be remembered that the contacts between England and Sicily were very frequent throughout the twelfth century. Many Englishmen held important posts at the Sicilian court; there were also close family relationships and frequent journeys between the two countries. As for York, the link with Sicily existed in a person of no less importance than Archbishop William Fitzherbert, later St. William of York. He was elected Archbishop of York in 1142 but his election was questioned on the grounds of alleged simony and strongly opposed by the Cistercians. In 1147 William was compelled to go to Rome and, through the intervention of St. Bernard, was suspended and then deposed by the Pope, Eugenius III. William took refuge in Sicily at the court of King Roger. Later he went to Winchester, where he was the guest of his uncle, Henry of Blois, Bishop of Winchester. In 1153, after the death of Eugenius III, William went to Rome to plead with Pope Anastasius IV for his reinstatement. The Cistercian Archbishop of York, Murdach, died in the same year and William was restored to his former office. He went back to England by way of Canterbury and Winchester and entered York on the 9th May, 1154. William was not long to enjoy his final triumph, for he died a month later and it was suspected that he was poisoned.

The fact of William's stay in Sicily, Winchester and York, combined with the artistic relationship between the York Virgin and the Winchester Psalter on the one hand, and Sicilian art on the other, seems more than a mere coincidence. Although William died so soon after his return to York, it was quite possible for him to have ordered an image of the Virgin to be carved, perhaps as a thanksgiving, supplying as a model a Sicilian work of art. Perhaps, on the other hand, the work was sponsored by one of those companions who were with him during his exile. Professor Wormald's dating of the Winchester Psalter to about 1150 coincides exactly with William's stay at Winchester and it is likely that while he was there, Sicilian works of art brought by him to England were copied by the illuminators of the Psalter.

The York Virgin is apparently executed in the local Tadcaster stone and there can therefore be no doubt that it is of local workmanship and in fact, some details are peculiar to English Romanesque sculpture of the mid-twelfth century. For instance, the treatment of the folds of the garment below her knee, shown by two concentric grooves, and those of the right leg, forming rhythmical curves, are found in otherwise stylistically unconnected work such as the Rood at Barking.   *Fig.* 65

This sculpture, in spite of its very damaged condition, still shows traces of a monumental, dignified composition and carving of high quality. The relief was originally made of twelve blocks of stone, of which only nine remain, and represents Christ on the Cross and the mourning figures of St. Mary and St. John the Evangelist. The sculpture is characterised by very firm outlines and rather stiff, angular folds of draperies, more appropriate in metal than in stone sculpture. One can indicate, for instance, the close parallel that exists between the treatment of folds at Barking and those of the figures of the apostles on the lead font at Wareham *Fig.* 66 in Dorset. The diaper pattern of the background of the Barking Rood, which gave rise to speculation about its thirteenth century date, is found frequently in Southern England between 1120 and 1160 and agrees well with the mid-century date of the rood.

The Byzantine influence which was such an important factor in the development of English Romanesque illumination from the second quarter of the twelfth century onwards, is best seen in the treatment of the human figure. It is no longer a mere symbolic representation but gives a far greater illusion of flesh and blood. This was brought about by the use of the Byzantine device of the so-called damped drapery, which clings to the body, revealing its shape and movement. A further characteristic of this device is the panel fold, which divides the surface of the draperies. The design of these narrow folds further emphasizes the structure of the human body. This method of painting human figures appeared for *Fig.* 68 the first time in England in the Bury Bible shortly before 1148 and about 1150 in the Winchester Psalter, two manuscripts which have already been mentioned in connection with the York Virgin.

An identical style translated, however, into a different *Fig.* 67 medium, is found in two panels preserved at Durham. These panels, carved in sandstone, less than three feet high, are divided horizontally into two scenes. They were found in the walls of the Canons' houses but, as Sir Alfred Clapham suggested, probably formed part of the original screen of the cathedral. This screen was carved with scenes from the life of Christ and the apostles. The two panels are only a small part of the whole screen and, as their subjects suggest, the cycle included representations seldom found in sculpture. The first panel shows the *Transfiguration*. In the upper part, Christ stands in the centre between Moses and Elias. In the lower, he appears to Peter, James and John as described in the Gospel of St. Matthew. The other panel shows two different incidents following the resurrection. The upper relief shows *Christ appearing to Mary Magdalen*. His appearance to two women returning from the sepulchre is shown in the lower.

Unfortunately, the heads of all the figures are missing and there is further damage to the reliefs but in spite of their unsatisfactory state of preservation, these panels are strikingly beautiful. The clarity of the composition and the subtlety of the modelling places them amongst the masterpieces of Romanesque sculpture. The date of these sculptures, sometimes given as about 1170, must be very close to the date of the Bury Bible, which, luckily, we know was executed before 1148. If we place the Durham reliefs between 1150 and 1160, we shall allow a sufficient lapse of time for the spread of the new style to the North and its adoption by local sculptors.

VI

The Yorkshire School

The Byzantine-influenced style of the York Virgin and the Durham screen was not, however, followed by the assimilation or further development of their style in the North of England. Contemporary with the creation of these two outstanding works, a vigorous new school of sculpture came to life in Yorkshire. The origin of the earliest style of this Yorkshire School is closely linked with the Southern School of the first half of the century, which originated at Canterbury. This southern style was transplanted to Durham about 1130 *Vol. I, Fig. 60* where it is seen in the decoration of the cathedral doorway and in the slightly later decoration of the capitals supported *Figs. 36, 37* by the caryatids of the chapter house.

In one of the churches directly influenced in its architecture by Durham, Selby Abbey in Yorkshire, there is a series of *Fig. 73* capitals in the nave, the earliest of which show an unmistakable derivation from the decorative style of the south, obviously transmitted from Durham. These capitals, judging from architectural evidence, date from about 1140. It should be remembered that the earliest capitals of the Southern School were carved with animal and foliage motives strictly subordi-*Vol. I, Fig. 47* nated to the shapes of the cushion capitals. Gradually this functional character of sculpture was replaced by more picturesque tendencies in which the decoration disregarded the shape of the capital and invaded its whole surface indiscriminately. It was at this stage of its development that the southern style was transmitted to Durham and thence to Selby.

In a little church at Brayton, about two miles from Selby, *Fig. 74* the chancel arch contains capitals closely related in their decoration to those at Selby. The cushion outlines of some of the capitals are still retained and their decoration is of an almost Southern School type. Next to these capitals are found others, carved by the same workshop and at the same time, on which the sculpture spreads freely over the whole surface in the true Yorkshire manner.

The date of the chancel arch must be fairly close to that of the Selby capitals and must thus be placed at about 1150. The north doorway at Brayton, built a year or two after the *Figs. 75, 76* chancel arch, shows a final break with the traditions of the Southern School. Here, the cushion shapes of the capitals are completely abandoned, and their decoration consists of an almost wild mixture of motives, floral, animal and human. The decoration spreads over on to the abaci, where side by side with the elegant foliage, archaic-looking interlacements are used. Above, the four orders of the arches include the chevron ornament, medallions, each containing a different figural subject, and beak-heads. The technique is very skilful and the style, in spite of the curious mixture of motives, has nothing hesitant about it.

The Brayton doorway is one of many surviving products of a school flourishing in Yorkshire during the whole of the third quarter of the twelfth century. The school consisted of many workshops, each with its individual characteristics, yet using a style of carving so similar that Yorkshire more than any other region, including Herefordshire, can claim to have established a regional style of sculpture.

York was undoubtedly the most important centre of the school. In the crypt of the Minster, built about 1160 by Archbishop Roger of Pont-l'Evêque, there are six free-standing, octagonal capitals, one of which is scalloped, another carved with eight caryatids supporting the abacus, while the remaining are tightly covered with foliage decoration, carved in flat relief. These capitals are one of the most elegant and *Figs. 77, 78* restrained examples of the Yorkshire School. There are several other important groups of sculpture in York produced by the school. The much restored doorway of St. Margaret's, Walmgate, brought there from the destroyed hospital of St. Nicholas, built about 1160, has deeply recessed orders with a great variety of motives: foliage, beak-heads and medallions. It is interesting to note that each voussoir is carved with a separate motive, the axes of which are parallel with the radii of the arches. This method of decorating arches, the radiating arches as they are called, was particularly popular in Western France and it was from there that this method was adopted in some churches of the Hereford-shire School, notably at Shobdon and Brinsop.

The indebtedness of the Yorkshire School to the sculpture of Western France, then united with England under Henry II, is unmistakable. The radiating voussoirs were used in almost every doorway of the school, Fishlake being a notable exception. For instance, the voussoirs discovered in York in 1941 and now preserved in the Yorkshire Museum are of this type. They combine the foliage decoration very similar in character to that on the capitals of the Minster crypt, with medallions like those at Brayton. At Alne we find a comparatively simple doorway with only two orders, but its decoration is remarkable for it contains one of the most comprehensive representations in sculpture of the animals of the Bestiaries which are, moreover, given inscriptions.

Figs. 79, 80

Figs. 81, 82

Perhaps the most striking analogy between the Yorkshire School and Western France is found at Barton-le-Street. The original Romanesque church there was destroyed in 1871, but its sculptural decoration was used in the new building. The original church had a richly carved chancel arch, two doorways and a corbel-table. This last is of a type very unusual in England; the individual corbels are joined by arches, in the apex of which are additional heads. This type of corbel-table is one of the most characteristic features of the sculpture of Western France, the best-known example being the church of Notre-Dame-la-Grande at Poitiers. If the corbel-table at Barton-le-Street was derived from Poitou, other elements in the decoration of this church have their source in pre-Conquest art. The flat carving on the label of the outer doorway of the porch, which was formerly the north doorway, represents animals with tails forming elaborate interlacements, a motive commonly used on the crosses of pre-Conquest times. This decoration of the label has no parallel in the Yorkshire School and is reminiscent of a doorway at Bradbourne in Derbyshire. The reliefs, which were originally placed on either side of the chancel arch at Barton-le-Street and are now built into the wall over the inner doorway of the porch, recall the drawings of the so-called Winchester School and their date has often been mistakenly thought to be pre-Conquest. Yorkshire was one of the most important centres of sculpture in Anglo-Saxon times and therefore it is not surprising to find in this region elements of pre-Conquest art surviving well into the twelfth century.

The south doorway of the church at Fishlake is a later Figs. 83, 84 work of the school, dating from about 1170. Each of the four orders of the doorway is carved with a different motive. The first is enriched with foliage, similar to that of the capitals of the York Minster crypt. On the second, we find small human heads carved in high relief, with a large leaf between each pair of heads. This decoration is a final development of the beak-head motive in which the leaf replaces the beak. The beak-head ornament was one of the most popular motives in Yorkshire but its form became gradually changed and went out of use about 1180. The third order of the doorway represents a hunting scene, carved in a strip-form along the whole length of the arch. This is an exquisite carving in which running hounds are shown with a sense of keen observation and some of the hunters have the lightness and elegance of Anglo-Saxon drawings. They are closely related to the figures on the reliefs at Barton-le-Street.

Some of the best sculptures of the Yorkshire School are found on the arch of the fourth order at Fishlake. The *Fig.* 84 medallions carved on it contain two seated figures each, probably the apostles and saints. The figures are greatly weathered but, in spite of this, they show a delicate modelling of the heads and draperies. The sculpture of the Yorkshire School was often highly decorative but seldom achieved the monumental quality which is present in the figure of this arch at Fishlake. The two figures of the Virtues fighting the

Vices carved at either end of this arch, have the charm and lightness of the hunters on the previous order.

In contrast to the radiating voussoirs of the first two orders of this doorway, the sculpture of the other two is placed parallel to the circumference of the arches. As it has already been pointed out, the first of these methods was derived from Western France. There are, however, a number of churches in Western France, particularly in the Charente district, *Fig.* 95 characterised by doorways decorated with the figures of the Virtues and Vices placed parallel to the circumference of the arches. Although the subject of the combat between the Virtues and the Vices, inspired by the poem *Psychomachia*, written by Prudentius, was very popular in medieval art as a whole, it was not common in English sculpture and the *Fig.* 96 other example of it at Malmesbury is also connected with Western France. Thus it is possible that this particular treatment of the sculpture at Fishlake, combined with a subject based on the *Psychomachia* was also derived from the French domains of Henry II. It should be added that tympana are as rare on the doorways of Yorkshire churches as they are in Western France.

The artistic production of the Yorkshire School must have been enormous. In addition to decorating churches, of which only a few are mentioned here, there are fonts, for example at Hutton Cranswick, and tomb-slabs such as the one at Conisborough, which are works of the school. In the early Romanesque period when Yorkshire was no doubt still suffering from the results of the destructive expedition of William the Conqueror in 1068, this region had little sculpture to offer. By the third quarter of the twelfth century, however, Yorkshire was undoubtedly the most prolific centre for sculpture in the country. It was also in this region that the most important works at the end of the Romanesque period were to be produced.

VII

Late Romanesque Sculpture

The Western French elements, which were so typical of the Yorkshire style, quite naturally appeared in other parts of England as well, the best known example being the main doorway of Rochester Cathedral. The radiating voussoirs of *Figs. 85, 86* this doorway are, as Prior and Gardner have already stated, so entirely Pointivin in character that they could have been executed by a sculptor from that region. The similarity between the voussoirs at Rochester and those at Notre-Dame-la-Grande at Poitiers, compelled these distinguished scholars to date Rochester to about 1180, the date given at that time to the Poitiers church. It has since been established that the date of the erection of this building was nearly fifty years earlier and it is therefore much more fitting to date the voussoirs of Rochester to about 1160, the approximate date of the completion of the nave. As previously pointed out, the Pointivin churches had no tympana over their doorways, though tympana were used over decorative blind niches, as at Parthenay-le-Vieux, mentioned in connection with the *Fig. 33* Herefordshire School. It would thus be surprising to find a sculptor from Poitiers carving a tympanum at Rochester and indeed he did not. The tympanum as well as the column-figures, representing Solomon and the Queen of Sheba, are later insertions, dating from about 1175.

The Rochester tympanum is stylistically close to the early Gothic tympana of the Ile-de-France, although iconographically it is of Burgundian origin. It represents *Christ in Majesty* in a mandorla, which is supported by two angels, and surrounded by the four symbols of the Evangelists. The column-figures are so weathered that they have lost practically all their artistic value. But they are important in showing the penetration of Gothic influences into England at the time of the rebuilding of Canterbury Cathedral choir by William of Sens. The Rochester figures may have been, carved by one of the Frenchmen who were working at Canterbury. It was, however, an isolated phenomenon, which did not alter the course of the development of Romanesque sculpture in England.

The influence of the sculpture of Western France must have been strong in Kent as it persisted until about 1180, the date of the churches at Barfreston and Patrixbourne. The two equestrian figures, fragments of which still stand in niches on the west front of Barfreston, are a direct imitation of the *Constantines* of Western France. The elaborately carved *Figs.*
87—91 doorways, friezes and other enrichments of this church show an extraordinary mixture of French motifs and the local style. This latter was derived from the Southern School and more particularly from Canterbury. The profusion of humorous subjects at Barfreston recalls the capitals of the crypt at Canterbury Cathedral and the manuscripts of the Canterbury School, dating from the first half of the twelfth century.

The most important decorative scheme in which the Western French influence is present is that of Malmesbury Abbey in Wiltshire. It is generally assumed that the building of the new church there was begun after the death of Bishop Roger of Salisbury, who unlawfully appropriated the abbey and its revenues in 1118 and held it until his death in 1139. The choir was built first but today it is a sad ruin. The nave was finished about 1175. Although Roger did not play a part in the building of the abbey, he is known to have built a castle at Malmesbury, subsequently pulled down by King Stephen. As has been suggested, some of the masons who worked for Roger at Old Sarum were later employed by his nephew, Bishop Alexander at Lincoln. It seems probable that these masons returned to Wiltshire when the west front of Lincoln was completed and worked at Malmesbury, for *Figs.* 45—43 we find here a few details of decoration that were earlier employed at Sarum and Lincoln.

Only a small fragment of the west doorway at Malmesbury survives but the south entrance to the nave, covered by a porch, although damaged, is still the glory of the church.

The porch contains two doorways, an outer one, composed of eight continuous orders and without a tympanum and the inner doorway of three orders, also continuous and enclosing a tympanum with *Christ in Majesty* in a mandorla supported by two angels. On the walls of the porch, connecting the two doorways, are set two tympana, each with six apostles and a flying angel above them.

Figs. 92, 93

This elaborate decorative scheme, although the work of more than one sculptor, is of one date and, judging from the position of the porch near the west end of the nave, must have been finished not long before the completion of the building. It should thus be dated at about 1160 to 1170. The porches with sculptural decorations on the side walls were, as far as we know, unknown in England but appear in such French churches as Moissac, Souillac, Conques and Ydes in South-Western France. It is difficult to say whether the idea of the Malmesbury porch was derived from these churches because in the iconography, composition and style, it had little in common with them. It is the sculpture of the Saintonge region of Western France that influenced Malmesbury. This is seen both in the figure sculpture and the ornament. One of the doorways of the church at Aulnay-de-Saintonge is a fairly *Fig.* 95 typical example of the style in this region in the second quarter of the twelfth century. This style is characterised by the plastic treatment of the elongated human body and the emphasis given to the rhythmical folds, marked by incised lines rather than by modelling. The Virtues trampling the Vices at Aulnay bear a certain resemblance to the figures with the same subject at Malmesbury and their relationship is further suggested by the ornament. The abacus of the doorway at Aulnay has an ornament composed of beaded bands forming a diamond-shaped pattern, which interlaces with two symmetrical scrolls. This is a comparatively simple design but the study of its distribution shows that it is extremely common in Western France and almost unknown elsewhere. At Malmesbury, however, this ornament and its *Fig.* 96 variants are used profusely.

41

Although the indebtedness of the sculpture of Malmesbury to that of Western France is a strong probability, its connections with English works should not be overlooked. First of all, the form of the doorways is typically English. The continuous orders of the doorways are more common in England than in any other country and were locally evolved. One can trace the development from doorways with only one continuous order, framed by orders with shafts, as at Southwell, to examples in which all orders are continuous and which are usually of a rather late date.

The Malmesbury tympana were once painted and gilded. The figures of the apostles show a late stage in the evolution of the style which originated at Ely. The examples of the intermediate stages of this style are the Majesty at Rouse Lench in Worcestershire and the apostles on the Lincoln frieze. The similarities between the Lincoln apostles and those at Malmesbury lie in the use of strained folds to cover the limbs, otherwise the treatment and the spirit of the two works are different, as can be expected in sculptures separated by about twenty years.

Figs. 62, 92

The Malmesbury apostles having been protected by the porch, are well preserved and are of an astounding quality. Their exaggerated gestures, the crossed legs of two of the figures, the heads vigorously turned to each other and the angel's widely stretched wings and crossed arms, give these compositions a dynamic quality which is further emphasized by the violent emotions expressed on their faces. These sculptures are inspired works of art that need not fear comparison with the best Romanesque achievements abroad.

The tympanum of the inner doorway exhibits a similar but softer style and is the work of a different sculptor. It is a real misfortune that the outer doorway is so badly weathered that none of the reliefs have escaped unharmed and some have even perished completely. The decoration consists here of alternating orders with ornamental and figural motives. The figures are enclosed by medallions, composed of intersecting, continuous beaded bands.

Most Romanesque sculptures in England were carved in advance, in the workshops of the sculptors, unless carving was added to an older structure already standing. At Malmesbury, however, two different methods were used. Small disagreements in the patterns of neighbouring stones *Fig. 96* on the outer doorway indicate that the stones were carved before they were put in position. The tympana with the apostles were, however, carved in position upon the ordinary *Fig. 93* ashlar facing. This use of two different methods of carving further proves that the tympana with the apostles were executed by a different sculptor from the one who carved the doorways.

The subjects of the medallion reliefs represent one of the most elaborate iconographical programmes of English Romanesque sculpture. The Old Testament scenes are arranged as types or figures of those of the New Testament. Below, the Virtues and Vices are engaged in combat. The *Fig. 96* figures, particularly in the scenes of Christ's Passion, are *Fig. 94* elongated and their forms made to fit the shapes of the medallions. Their gestures are so expressive that even today, in spite of their mutilations, they are deeply moving.

After Malmesbury, much of the late Romanesque sculpture is an anti-climax. The two fonts at Stanton Fitzwarren in *Fig. 97* Wiltshire and at Southrop in Gloucestershire, which are the *Fig. 98* work of one sculptor, look lifeless, though they have great decorative merits. The symbolical subjects carved on them, like the Virtues and Vices and the Ecclesia and Synagogue show, however, a greater iconographical sophistication than most of the contemporary fonts.

At the close of the twelfth century, in several parts of the country, there were workshops specialising in the carving of fonts. The most outstanding of them were the workshops of Norfolk, the Chiltern Hills and Cornwall. The leading examples of these groups of fonts are found at Shernborne *Figs. 99,* (Norfolk), Great Kimble (Bucks) and Bodmin (Cornwall). *100* *Fig. 101* The approximate dates of the activities of these workshops are, in Norfolk between 1160 to 1180, in the Chiltern Hills between 1170 and 1190 and in Cornwall between 1190 and the end of the first quarter of the thirteenth century. The shapes of the fonts and their decorations differ greatly from district to district but they have one thing in common, a great elaboration of form and richness of ornament. The Norfolk fonts derive their rectangular bowls supported by five shafts from the Tournai type, but their decoration is thoroughly English in its love of interlacements. The beautifully proportioned, chalice-shaped and fluted fonts of the Chiltern Hills group use for their decoration foliage motives similar to those in contemporary manuscripts. The Cornish fonts, also chalice-shaped but with four shafts added to the bowl and with angels' heads carved instead of capitals, show a very skilful carving technique. Their decoration, although still Romanesque already shows a transitional style in its motifs.

The development towards an ever-increasing complexity of form and decoration is well illustrated by a late twelfth *Fig. 102* century font at Stafford. It takes the form of four clustered bowls with animals climbing up between them. The base is even more complicated: four lions supporting the bowl rest on one-headed but two-bodied monsters.

This tendency towards elaboration can be found in the decoration of many late twelfth century churches. The west *Fig. 103* front of Tutbury in Staffordshire can serve as an example. Here the desire to impress by richness rather than by the quality of the decoration is painfully obvious. Occasionally, however, the results are quite happy. The well-known church at Iffley near Oxford, built between 1175 and 1182, has two *Fig. 104* doorways. The west doorway must be one of the last examples of the use of the beak-head ornament, but at the same time no other exists where this ornament is used to greater advantage. The south doorway has some exquisite *Figs.* *105-107* details carved on capitals and jambs—birds, sirens, monsters, fighting horsemen and a female centaur suckling her young. The relief is crisp, full of vitality and has a note of humour. Inside the church, in the chancel, the shafts are enriched with carved flowers and a few figure subjects, amongst them a

44

delightful bird guarding its nest. The boss, which joins the *Fig.* 108 chevron ribs of the chancel, is carved with grotesque heads and a dragon. *Fig.* 109

Carved bosses were the innovation of the twelfth century. One of the earliest, dating from before 1150 is found in Peterborough Cathedral, at that time an abbey. By the end of the twelfth century this type of decoration was well established, but of course its greatest popularity and prodigious development was to come in the Gothic period. The Romanesque bosses are truly functional in their decoration. This is admirably expressed at Elkstone Church in Gloucestershire dating from about 1180, where a boss was given the form *Fig.* 110 of a head with four mouths from which the ribs protrude; to increase the impression of security a belt is fastened across the boss.

VIII

The Transitional Style

There are comparatively few well-preserved sculptures from the last two decades of the twelfth century and thus it is difficult to get a clear picture of the changes that were taking place in this vital period of transition. We know that the French influences on sculpture, resulting from the rebuilding of the choir of Canterbury in the Gothic style by William of Sens after the fire of 1174, were neither wide nor very significant. This was no doubt due to the comparatively modest scale of the sculptural decoration at Canterbury, limited to the capitals only.

There exist two fragments of late twelfth century Canterbury reliefs, one preserved in the Cathedral Library there, the other in the Victoria and Albert Museum. They formed part of a single decorative scheme, possibly of the west front of the Almonry Chapel. Each of the reliefs represents a half-figure of a prophet enclosed by a quatrefoil. There is nothing markedly French in these reliefs. They show rather a certain classical element, perhaps derived, like the English manuscripts of the period, from Byzantine sources. There are still some Romanesque conventions visible but the body is more substantial, the drapery has lost its pattern-like quality and gives the impression of a heavy material, while the softly rounded folds are logical in their flow. In the faces, the Romanesque stylisation is replaced by relatively individual modelling. In these reliefs new possibilities for sculpture are emerging.

Fig. 111

The fulfilment of the promise embodied in these two reliefs is not to be found in Kent. An interesting shaft at Bobbing near Sittingbourne, although not unconnected with the Canterbury reliefs, returned to a more Romanesque, formal treatment of the figures and the draperies.

Fig. 112

In the West of England, classical tendencies in sculpture were also present. The two panels of the octagonal lavatory

46

in the cloister of the Cluniac Priory at Much Wenlock are *Figs.* 113, 114 a case in point. One of the panels represents two prophets or saints standing under arcades. The figures are squat with large heads. The other panel, of which only the lower part is finished, shows the *Calling of St. Peter*. The group is enclosed by a trefoiled arch. The panels are clearly provincial works but not without some merit. They are related to the fonts at Stanton Fitzwarren and at Southrop, and were probably *Figs.* 97, 98 later products of the same workshop. One feels that the convincing attitudes of the figures and their grouping were copied from a superior model, but in the process the figures were made shorter and the classical draperies lost their logic and became a mere pattern.

By far the most important group of sculptures of the late Romanesque period in England is found in the North. A capital in the Yorkshire Museum at York dating from about 1180, carved in high relief and showing human figures fighting with monsters is interesting as it shows that at about that time the activities of the Yorkshire School, at least in York, came to an end. The fragment of a tympanum in the same museum and a large slab carved with an elaborate representation of *Doom* kept in the crypt of York Minster, are works of the very end of the century. They are vigorous in both modelling and composition, and indicate excellent observation of movement and expression.

But a more significant style is found in a fragment of a small statuette, found recently at Bridlington Priory in Yorkshire and now preserved in the Victoria and Albert Museum. The fragment shows the lower half of a figure, *Figs.* 115, 116 the whole originally measuring about one foot in height. The figure is carved in the round but the back is left plain, an indication that the statuette was placed against a background, possibly a niche.

The artistic quality of the Bridlington statuette is of the highest order; even in its fragmentary state it is of arresting beauty. The pose of the figure, leaning slightly forward suggests that perhaps it formed part of a group and the

Annunciation or the *Visitation* scenes inevitably come to one's mind.

Bridlington was an Augustinian Priory and a centre of learning of some repute. As it happens, we have two Psalters dating from about 1170—1180 which, from the peculiarities of their calendars, must be attributed to an Augustinian house in Yorkshire. One is preserved in the Hunterian Library of Glasgow University, the other in the Royal Library in Copenhagen. The style of the Glasgow Psalter developed from that which is best represented by the Bury Bible; in the Glasgow Psalter, however, the Byzantine drapery was transformed into an extravagant pattern. In this manuscript we find numerous and striking parallels for the somewhat illogical fold of the outer garment of the Bridlington statuette. In the Copenhagen Psalter the style is robust and is much more in keeping with Byzantine traditions. The *Visitation* scene in this Psalter makes an extraordinarily close comparison with the Bridlington fragment and suggests two conclusions: first, that both came from one artistic centre, namely from Bridlington and secondly, that their dates are contemporary, which places the sculpture between 1170 and 1180.

Fig. 117

Figs. 118-125

The life-size statues from St. Mary's Abbey at York, now in the Yorkshire Museum, have many points of contact with the Bridlington statuette. Ten of the figures have so far been recovered, seven by excavations, two were re-used in another church at York and the last was built into the bridge at Clifton. All these figures were attached to shafts, traces of which are still visible on their backs and were true column-figures. Two of them can be identified, *Moses* by his Tables of the Law and *St. John the Baptist* by his Lamb. One can presume, therefore, that the series represented Christ's forerunners, as they appeared on the façades of French cathedrals, for instance, at Saint-Denis, Chartres, Rheims and Amiens. There can be little doubt that, in fact, the York figures were strongly influenced by the monumental art of the Ile-de-France.

The closest parallels for the York statues are found at Chartres and Laon. At Chartres the column-figures of the central doorways of both transepts, dating from the first decade of the thirteenth century, exhibit a general similarity of modelling to the York figures. The most likely date for them is the second decade of the thirteenth century. From the example of Bridlington, we know that carving in the round was already practised in Yorkshire about 1170—80 and that the classical style, derived from Byzantine sources, was then applied to stone sculpture with great success.

The most striking feature of the York figures is the classical element in the treatment of their draperies. If the faces of some of the York figures are particularly close to those at Laon, their draperies are more classical than anything that is known to us in the Ile-de-France, except the works of the so-called Master of the Antique Figures at Rheims, who worked there between 1211 and 1230.

The classicism of the York figures might have been a French importation, for it is present in many early thirteenth century works of the Ile-de-France. If so, it was certainly strengthened by the classical elements present in England since the second quarter of the twelfth century and derived from Byzantine models. This applies mostly to manuscript painting but, in some cases, also to sculpture. The North of England can boast such outstanding examples of this classical trend as the York Virgin, the Durham screen and the Bridlington statuette. Thus it seems natural that here in the North, column-figures of French origin were transformed in the spirit of these local traditions.

The doorway of St. Mary's must have been as impressive as its French prototypes. Four voussoirs, preserved in the Yorkshire Museum, were probably part of its arches. They are carved with scenes from the New Testament. The *Fig.* 126 column-figures still bore traces of their original colour when they were discovered, indicating that in this case, as in most medieval sculpture, stone was richly painted and gilded. Except for a very modest example at Rochester, there are no doorways preserved in England with column-figures as their chief decoration. The statues at York perhaps suggest that there were originally more of these doorways but, like those at York, they were destroyed at the time of the Reformation.

The York statues are transitional in style but although at least partly inspired by French early Gothic art, they can be conveniently included in a survey of Romanesque sculpture because they still have a great deal in common with the style of the latter half of the twelfth century. In fact, they have more in common with such sculptures as the Bridlington statuette than with the early Gothic works of the thirteenth century at Peterborough or Wells.

At Lincoln there are two figures carved in the round and *Fig.* 128 placed in niches over the central doorway. Their heads are restorations and it is probably due to the misleading character of these heads that the figures have been so far overlooked. They are, however, important examples of the late twelfth or early thirteenth century transitional style.

In the West of England the doorways of the Lady Chapel *Figs.* 129, 130 at Glastonbury show an even more advanced stage of transition. These doorways are often uncritically dated to about 1185, the date of the building of the chapel, but it is obvious that the carvings were added *in situ* at a later date and, in fact, one doorway has never been finished. They are undoubtedly early thirteenth century works with a few Romanesque conventions in their figure style but are already purely Gothic in the treatment of the foliage. The remains *Fig.* 133 of the cloister at Bridlington Priory, although different in style, represents a similar stage in which Romanesque stylisation mixes with the new Gothic naturalism.

The change of style is admirably illustrated by a relief of the Majesty with the symbols of the Evangelists in St. Mary-*Fig.* 131 the-Less at Durham. This relief was inspired by a fresh naturalism and the remarkable similarity it exhibits to the *Fig.* 132 celebrated Westminster Psalter in the British Museum proves how widespread was this movement.

The development of English sculpture from the capital with the *Judgment of Solomon* at Westminster Abbey to the York figures covers about seventy years, a length of time equal to that which separated the Westminster capital from the Norman Conquest. The evolution of sculpture in this earlier period was rather slow, hesitant and contacts with artistic centres abroad were rare. It was from the end of the first half of the twelfth century that English sculptors became aware of the tremendous activities in this field on the Continent and they freely drew inspiration from it. They seldom copied slavishly and rather enriched earlier English traditions with new forms and ideas derived from abroad. Foreign works of art were brought to England and sometimes even foreign artists seem to have been employed. The variety of style in English sculpture of the later Romanesque period is great because so many different models inspired it. Political expansion brought England into particularly close contact with Aquitaine, although artistic relationships with other parts of France, with Flanders and with Italy were equally fruitful. Above all, the Byzantine influence, which swept across Western Europe and was so marked in English twelfth century art, introduced those classical elements which Byzantine art inherited from late antiquity.

If a generalization is permissible, it can be said that the development of English sculpture was characterized by a gradual abandonment of linear qualities in favour of plastic ones, with a corresponding change from forms used as decorative, often abstract patterns, into a new conception of sculpture in which figures play a leading role and their existence is not merely symbolical but also physical.

It is a common belief, particularly in England, that English medieval sculpture is far inferior to contemporary sculpture on the Continent. It is all too easily forgotten, however, that owing to the peculiarly English institution of cathedral-abbeys, their destruction following the dissolution of the monasteries deprived England of many of her most important medieval monuments. In addition to this, the iconoclastic thoroughness of the puritans of the seventeenth century inflicted irreparable damage to much religious art, particularly figure subjects.

That is the reason why, in dealing with English medieval sculpture, so many damaged objects have to suffice while in other countries well-preserved sculptures give an impression of greater richness and accomplishment. To assess the English contribution to Romanesque art is therefore difficult. This book has been written in the hope that it may contribute a little to this much-neglected subject, and may help also to change the attitude, put so bluntly by a writer in an article on Kilpeck published in a learned journal, " The Briton could only copy and coarsen, where the French would create."

DESCRIPTIVE NOTES TO PLATES

1. LONDON, WESTMINSTER ABBEY; detail of capital. *Circa* 1140.
   A large capital kept in the triforium of the Abbey; it is not known to which part of the structure this capital originally belonged. At one time it must have been used as building material, for three of its surfaces have been cut away to make them flat. The subject of the face that survives practically intact is the *Judgment of Solomon*.

2. AVINGTON CHURCH (BERKSHIRE); font. *Circa* 1140.
   The font is decorated with eleven arcades containing two pairs of figures and nine single ones. Some figures are those of ecclesiastics and include a bishop with a two-cornered mitre. The style is derived from Reading (see Vol. I, Fig. 61), but is more plastic, though at the same time strikingly provincial.

3. DARENTH (KENT), ST. MARGARET'S; font. *Circa* 1140.
   The two arcades which are illustrated here show the *Rite of Baptism* and a king. The style of the carving, in comparison with early Romanesque works, shows an increasing feeling for plasticity. The quality of the carving is as provincial as in the previous example.

4. AVEBURY (WILTSHIRE), ST. JAMES'; font. *Circa* 1140.
   The arcade with intersecting arches covers the lower part of the font. Above is the illustration of Psalm XC, 13: *Thou shalt tread upon the lion and adder*, in which Christ is trampling on two beasts.
   The foliage and a bird cover the rest of the surface. The relief is flat and the treatment highly stylised.

5. ALPHINGTON (DEVON), ST. MICHAEL'S; font. *Circa* 1140.
   One of two fonts carved by the same sculptor, the other being at Porchester in Hampshire. The arcade is similar to the previous example (Fig. 4) while the upper part of the font is decorated with a scroll and human figures fighting monsters.

6—7. COLESHILL (WARWICKSHIRE), ST. PETER AND ST. PAUL; font. *Circa* 1150.
   The scene of the *Crucifixion* is the principal subject of the decoration of this font. The rest of the surface is carved with arcades framing scrolls of foliage alternating with figures of saints. The *Crucifixion*, enclosed by a circular glory, is strikingly close to that on the stained glass window at Châlons-sur-Marne, dating from between 1145—1155 (L. Grodecki). The figures on the font were copied from a pattern-book so faithfully that individual pen-strokes were repeated in stone.

8. DEERHURST (GLOUCESTERSHIRE), PRIORY OF HOLY TRINITY AND ST. MARY; label stop of tower arch. *Tenth century*.
   One of a pair of wolves' heads of a distinctly Scandinavian character.

9. **LONDON, VICTORIA AND ALBERT MUSEUM**; detail of an arch from **Reading Abbey** (Berkshire). *Circa* 1130.

Probably the earliest existing example of the beak-head ornament. In its treatment and character it is based on pre-Conquest sculpture, such as the previous example.

10. **OXFORD, ST. EBBE'S**; arch of west doorway. *Circa* 1150.

A detail of the original doorway now set against the west wall. The connection with pre-Conquest sculpture is here emphasized by the use of a muzzled beak-head resembling the muzzled heads of "hog-backs," coped tomb-slabs of the Anglo-Saxon period.

11. **BARFORD (OXFORDSHIRE), ST. MICHAEL'S**; detail of north doorway. *Circa* 1150.

The beak-head ornament applied here to the arches and shafts is one of the purest and most harmonious examples in the country.

12—13. **BISHOP'S TEIGNTON (DEVON), ST. JOHN THE BAPTIST'S**; details of west doorway. *Third quarter of the twelfth century.*

An example of a highly elaborate treatment of the beak-head ornament. The beak-heads alternate with grotesque heads and the roll-moulding is covered with grapes. On the right, instead of a beak-head, is a bird in profile with a grape in its beak.

14—17. **NORTHAMPTON, ST. PETER'S**; capitals. *Circa* 1150.

The capitals of St. Peter's were discovered under the whitewash in 1839, hence their good state of preservation. The carvings are exceedingly flat. The chief motives of decoration are animals and birds with an occasional human figure enclosed by scrolls of foliage. Some of the leaves are reminiscent of the feather-like acanthus of the borders of the pre-Conquest illuminations of the Winchester School, others were obviously influenced by goldsmiths' technique.

18. **NORTHAMPTON, ST. PETER'S**; tomb-slab. *Circa* 1150.

A highly successful product of the local workshop, which was responsible for the decoration of the capitals (see Figs. 14—17) and the west front of the church of St. Peter's, as well as some fonts in the neighbourhood.

19. **KILPECK (HEREFORDSHIRE), ST. MARY AND ST. DAVID**; south doorway. *Circa* 1150.

One of the most accomplished works of the Herefordshire School. The vine-scroll of the tympanum is commonly interpreted as *The Tree of Life* but in fact has no symbolic significance. The design was evolved from early twelfth century tympana in Gloucestershire and Herefordshire carved with purely decorative leaves.

20. **KILPECK**; detail of south doorway.

A similar treatment of a figure intertwining with thin scrolls of foliage is found in a number of works of the Herefordshire School, notably at Shobdon, Leominster and on the font at Eardisley (Fig. 25),

21. KILPECK; detail of shaft of chancel arch. *Circa* 1150.
The figure of St. Peter is one of the six apostles carved on the shafts. This treatment was an imitation of the shafts of the *Puerta da las Platerias* at Compostela.

22—24. KILPECK; voussoirs of south doorway.

25. EARDISLEY (HEREFORDSHIRE), ST. MARY MAGDA-LEN'S; detail of font. *Circa* 1150.

26. KILPECK; corbel on west front. *Circa* 1150.
One of the five corbels at Kilpeck carved in the form of a dragon's head, based on a Viking model (see Fig. 27). Similar heads are found on the Norman Tower at Bury St. Edmunds; they are, however, the work of L. N. Cottingham, who restored the tower in 1846, the year in which he also restored Kilpeck !

27. LONDON, GUILDHALL MUSEUM; Viking comb. Bone. *Eleventh century*.

28. CASTLE FROME (HEREFORDSHIRE), ST. MICHAEL'S; detail of font. *Circa* 1150.
The head of one of the three crouching figures supporting the font is typical of the Herefordshire School (see Fig. 29).

29. KILPECK; corbel on west front.

30. CASTLE FROME; detail of font.
The scene of the *Baptism of Christ* conceived also as representation of the Holy Trinity, with Christ in the River Jordan and the hand of God and the dove of the Holy Ghost above.

31. BRINSOP (HEREFORDSHIRE), ST. GEORGE'S; tympanum. *Circa* 1150.
The patron saint of the church carved on this tympanum is a copy of a *Constantine* in Western France (see Fig. 33).

32. STRETTON SUGWAS (HEREFORDSHIRE), ST. MARY MAGDALEN'S; tympanum. *Circa* 1150.
Samson and the lion on this tympanum are, like the previous example, derived from a Western French model.

33. PARTHENAY-LE-VIEUX (DEUX-SÈVRES); west front of church. *Circa* 1120.
The tympana with the *Constantine* and *Samson and the lion*, which were copied by a Herefordshire sculptor on the two previous tympana.

34. STOTTESDON (SHROPSHIRE), ST. MARY'S; font. *Circa* 1160.
This font was a work of the Herefordshire School but exhibits a more restrained style than the majority of the sculptures of this school.

35. CHADDESLEY CORBETT (WORCESTERSHIRE), ST. CASSIAN'S; font. *Circa* 1160.

One of the most beautifully proportioned font of the Herefordshire school.

36—37. DURHAM CATHEDRAL; caryatids from chapter house. *Circa* 1140.

Two of the series of caryatids supporting capitals and the ribs of the vaulting, which originally sprung from the capitals.

38—39. WINCHESTER CATHEDRAL; font. *Third quarter of the twelfth century*.

Two sides of the Tournai font showing the story of St. Nicholas. The remaining Tournai fonts in England are at East Meon, at St. Mary Bourne, at St. Michael's, Southampton, in Lincoln Cathedral, at Thornton Curtis, at St. Peter's, Ipswich, and in the Ipswich Museum.

40. SALISBURY MUSEUM: capital from Old Sarum Cathedral. *Third quarter of the twelfth century*.

The capital is made of Tournai marble and was imported to England ready-made.

41. ELY CATHEDRAL; tomb-slab. *Third quarter of the twelfth century*.

One of the two tomb-slabs brought from Tournai to England, the other example being at Bridlington Priory.

42. SALISBURY MUSEUM; top of gable from Old Sarum Cathedral. *Circa* 1140.

The gable is surmounted by a pair of lions of a grotesque character.

43. SALISBURY MUSEUM; fragment of a doorway from Old Sarum Cathedral. *Circa* 1140.

Variant of the beak-head ornament applied to a shaft.

44. LINCOLN CATHEDRAL; detail of central doorway. *Circa* 1145.

One of the beak-heads decorating the shafts of the doorway, perhaps by a sculptor from Old Sarum.

45. SALISBURY MUSEUM; head, probably from apex of arch from Old Sarum Cathedral. *Circa* 1140.

46. MALMESBURY ABBEY (WILTSHIRE); head at apex of nave arcade. *Circa* 1160.

This sculpture is so strikingly similar to the previous example that their common authorship seems very probable. The Malmesbury head is more plastic and the features more exaggerated, a change of style quite possible in works separated by about twenty years.

47. LINCOLN CATHEDRAL; detail of central doorway. *Circa* 1145.

The label stop has the form of a head not unconnected with pre-Conquest art (see Fig. 8).

48. MALMESBURY ABBEY; label stop of nave arcade. *Circa* 1160.
   In comparison with the previous example, a change has occurred in the treatment of the label stops similar to that noticed in connection with the heads, illustrated as Figs. 45 and 46.

49. LINCOLN CATHEDRAL; shafts of central doorway. *Circa* 1145.

50. LINCOLN CATHEDRAL; capital of north doorway. *Circa* 1145.
   An acanthus capital of French inspiration and probably the work of a foreign sculptor.

51. SAINT-DENIS CATHEDRAL; capital in narthex. *Between* 1137 *and* 1140.
   This capital is placed high up in a dark narthex and is therefore only summarily carved. It shows, however, a strong resemblance in design to the previous example.

52. LINCOLN CATHEDRAL; detail of shaft of central doorway; *Circa* 1145.

53. SAINT-DENIS CATHEDRAL; detail of shaft of north doorway of west front. *Between* 1137 *and* 1140.
   Another instance of the similarity of detail between Saint-Denis and Lincoln (Fig. 52).

54—55. LINCOLN CATHEDRAL; details of central doorway. *Circa* 1145.

56. SAINT-DENIS CATHEDRAL; detail of south doorway of west front. *Between* 1137 *and* 1140.

57. LINCOLN CATHEDRAL; detail of frieze. *Circa* 1145.
   The relief represents *Cain and Abel* ; a similar scene can be found in the eleventh century Pentateuch in the British Museum (Cotton MS. Claudius B.IV). The hand with a flask containing blood is probably the illustration of St. Augustine's Commentary on the Psalms, in which he draws a parallel between the blood of Abel and that of Christ. This relief has usually been interpreted as Adam and Eve at work.
   The style of the relief is closely connected with the sculpture of Saint-Denis.

58. SAINT-DENIS CATHEDRAL; figures of inner arch of north doorway. *Between* 1137 *and* 1140.

59. LINCOLN CATHEDRAL; detail of frieze. *Circa* 1145.
   Noah leaving the Ark. The style of this relief, too, shows an indebtedness to Saint-Denis.

60. LINCOLN CATHEDRAL; detail of frieze. *Circa* 1145.
   Noah building the Ark.

61. LINCOLN CATHEDRAL ; detail of frieze, parable of *Dives and Lazarus. Circa* 1145.

62. **LINCOLN CATHEDRAL**; detail of frieze, ? Apostles. *Circa* 1145.

63. **LINCOLN CATHEDRAL** ; detail of frieze, *Harrowing of Hell* and *Doom. Circa* 1145.

   The three figures to the left of the *Harrowing of Hell* are nineteenth century restorations.

64. **YORK MINSTER**; Virgin and Child. ? 1154.

   The relief is in local stone but based on a Byzantine model, probably brought by St. William of York from Sicily.

65. **BARKING ABBEY (ESSEX)**; detail of Rood; St. John. *Circa* 1150.

   It is probable that the rood was part of a bigger composition, for there are many fragments built into the Curfew Tower and the present church, which are decorated with the diaper ornament similar to that used for the background of this relief. The technique of carving on small panels joined together recalls the Chichester reliefs (see Volume I, Figs. 80—82). The style of the Barking Rood is, however, more connected with the next example.

66. **WAREHAM (DORSET), ST. MARY'S**; detail of lead font. *Circa* 1150.

   The figures on the lead font have stiff, angular draperies appropriate to the material from which they are made.

67. **DURHAM CATHEDRAL**; relief of original screen. *Between* 1150 *and* 1160.

   Christ appears to St. Mary Magdalen (*Noli me tangere*) and, below, to the women returning from the sepulchre.

68. **CAMBRIDGE, CORPUS CHRISTI COLLEGE**; Bible of Bury St. Edmunds (MS. 2, fol. 94r). *Before* 1148.

   Moses and Aaron addressing the Israelites and, below, Moses establishing the law on unclean beasts. This manuscript, executed under strong Byzantine influence, shows a style parallel to that of the Durham relief (Fig. 67).

69. **LENTON (NOTTINGHAMSHIRE), HOLY TRINITY**; font. *Third quarter of the twelfth century.*

   The font was formerly in the Cluniac Priory at Lenton. It is richly carved and has some traces of the original colour. The subjects include the *Baptism of Christ*, the *Raising of Lazarus*, and the three *Marys at the Sepulchre*. The style of the carvings has no parallel in England. The late Sir Alfred Clapham believed it to be based on Spanish models.

70. a, b, **BRIGHTON (SUSSEX), ST. NICHOLAS'**; detail of font. *Third quarter of the twelfth century.*

   Very appropriately some of the subjects on this font tell the story of the patron saint of the church. Others depict the *Baptism of Christ* and the *Last Supper*. Stylistically, as the previous example, this font stands apart from current sculpture in England. The font has been slightly recut in 1853.

71—72. BRIDEKIRK (CUMBERLAND), ST. BRIDGET'S; font.
Third quarter of the twelfth century.
The font is elaborately decorated with the scene of the *Baptism of Christ*, symbolical beasts and foliage scrolls. Two remarkable features of this font deserve particular attention. One is the runic inscription so astonishing in the twelfth century. The inscription gives the name of the sculptor as *Richard*. The other unusual detail is the little figure of the sculptor himself, in the bottom left-hand corner of Fig. 72; he is shown carving the foliage of the font.

73. SELBY (YORKSHIRE), ABBEY OF ST. MARY AND ST. GERMAN; capital of nave. *Circa* 1140.
The foliage decoration of the capital was based on the style of the Southern School.

74. BRAYTON (YORKSHIRE), ST. WILFRID'S; capitals of chancel arch. *Circa* 1150.
The twin capital shows a clear connection with the Southern School (see Vol. I, Fig. 48), while the other capital has a distinct Yorkshire character, which is further developed on the doorway of this church (Fig. 76).

75—76. BRAYTON; details of south doorway. *Circa* 1150.
This doorway has all the characteristics of the Yorkshire School and was probably one of its earliest works.

77—78. YORK MINSTER; capitals of crypt. *Circa* 1160.
A more restrained style of the Yorkshire School confined only to foliage motives.

79—80. YORK, YORKSHIRE MUSEUM: voussoirs of doorway found at York. *Circa* 1160.
The foliage decorating the roll-moulding of these voussoirs is similar to that on the Minster capitals.

81—82. ALNE (YORKSHIRE), ST. MARY'S; details of south doorway. *Circa* 1160.
The subjects carved on the outer order of this doorway are the animals from the Bestiaries with inscriptions explaining their meanings. Those on Fig. 82 are: *Vulpis*, the fox pretending to be dead, *Panthera*, the panther with a dragon facing it, and *A(qui)la*, the eagle. The medallions of the inner order include an *Agnus Dei*, a few Signs of the Zodiac and one representation of the Labours of the Months.

83—84. FISHLAKE (YORKSHIRE), ST. CUTHBERT'S; details of south doorway. 1160—1170.
One of the most accomplished works of the Yorkshire School.

85—86. ROCHESTER CATHEDRAL; west doorway. *Circa* 1160 with later insertions.
The original doorway consisted of the richly carved voussoirs in the Pointevin style. The tympanum and the column-figures were added some fifteen years later and were inspired by the early Gothic sculpture of the Ile-de-France.

87—90. BARFRESTON (KENT), ST. MARY'S; details of south doorway. *Circa* 1180.

The decoration of the doorway is the last example of the style initiated in the first half of the century at Canterbury (see Vol. I, Figs. 49—57). The love of fabulous and humorous subjects so typical of Canterbury, found its fullest expression at Barfreston. Even the Majesty on the tympanum is surrounded by fabulous monsters. Although a few details of the decoration already foreshadow the Gothic style, the spirit is still wholly Romanesque.

91. BARFRESTON; capital of north doorway. *Circa* 1180.

92. MALMESBURY (WILTSHIRE), ABBEY OF ST. MARY; tympanum on east wall of porch. 1160—1170.

This tympanum is part of a bigger composition, the centre of which is the tympanum over the inner doorway, representing *Christ in Majesty*. The tympanum illustrated here and the other on the opposite side of the porch, represent the apostles. The flying angel above each group carries a scroll, which, when the whole was painted, undoubtedly had an inscription. Traces of colour and gilding still exist. The whole composition was meant to depict the glory of Christ and His disciples at the Last Judgement.

The treatment of the sitting figures with the strained folds over their limbs should be compared to that of the figures of the Lincoln frieze, which are some twenty years earlier (Fig. 62), as well as to the sculptures of some Western French churches (Fig. 95). As the Chichester reliefs (see Vol. I, Figs. 80—82) were the culmination of the development of Romanesque sculpture in England in the first half of the twelfth century, so the sculpture of Malmesbury holds a similar place in the second half of the century.

93. MALMESBURY; detail of tympanum on west wall of porch. 1160—1170.

The deep emotional content of the figures is vividly expressed by the gestures of the apostles, their heads ecstatically turned to each other and even by the deeply undercut folds of their draperies, making strong contrasts of light and shade.

94. MALMESBURY ; detail of outer doorway : *Entombment of Christ.* 1160—1170.

Two beaded bands form oval-shaped medallions, which contain small scenes carved with astonishing delicacy and often, as in the relief illustrated here, with dramatic power.

95. AULNAY - DE - SAINTONGE (CHARENTE - INFÉRIEURE), SAINT-PIERRE; detail of west doorway. *Second quarter of the twelfth century.*

The combat between the Virtues and Vices, inspired by the *Psychomachia*, the poem of Prudentius, was one of the favourite subjects of decoration on the churches of Western France. The Virtues are shown victorious, trampling on the fallen bodies of the Vices.

96. MALMESBURY; detail of outer doorway. 1160—1170.

Although the poem of Prudentius was well known in England, it was seldom illustrated in sculpture. It is interesting to note that " the finest of the English manuscripts of the *Psychomachia* " (Wormald) is a late tenth century copy, which belonged, in the Middle Ages, to Malmesbury Abbey. It is now in Corpus Christi College, Cambridge (MS. 23). The stylistic links of the Malmesbury reliefs, illustrating the *Psychomachia* show, however, that this subject was inspired not by English manuscript illustrations, but by the sculpture of Western France. The indebtedness of Malmesbury to Western France is further confirmed by the similarity of ornament. Compare, for instance, the band of ornament to the right of the medallions on Fig. 96 with the decoration on the abacus at Aulnay (Fig. 95).

97. STANTON FITZWARREN (WILTSHIRE), ST. LEONARD'S; font. *Circa* 1180.

Under ten trefoiled arches are represented eight Virtues, the *Ecclesia* and a *Cherubim*. In our illustration is seen the *Cherubim*, a six-winged figure with a sword and *Largitas* trampling on *Avaricia*.

98. SOUTHROP (GLOUCESTERSHIRE), ST. PETER'S; font. *Circa* 1180.

This font came from the same workshop as that at Stanton Fitzwarren. It has not only basically the same ornament but the subjects carved under the arcades are very similar. There are only eight arches at Southrop compared with ten at Stanton Fitzwarren and thus the number of Virtues represented is reduced to five, the remaining subjects being : Moses, the *Ecclesia* and the Synagogue. These three figures are illustrated in our photograph. In the spandrels of the arches are the mansions of the New Jerusalem.

99. SHERNBORNE (NORFOLK), ST. PETER AND ST. PAUL; font. *Circa* 1170.

One of the group of late twelfth century Norfolk fonts. Other examples include fonts at Toftrees, Castle Rising, Sculthorpe, South Wootton and Preston. Figural motives are comparatively rare on these fonts, although at Shernborne there is an inconspicuous representation of the Temptation scene.

100. GREAT KIMBLE (BUCKINGHAMSHIRE), ST. NICHOLAS'; font. *Circa* 1180.

Late twelfth century fonts of the Chiltern Hills region show a great similarity of form and decoration. They are characterised by cup-shaped, fluted bowls and the bases have the form of inverted scalloped capitals. The best examples of the group are found at Little and Great Missenden, Bledlow, Buckland, Houghton Regis, Weston Turville and Aylesbury. The font at Great Kimble has a band of ornament resembling those on the fonts at Stanton Fitzwarren and Southrop (Figs. 97—98).

101. BODMIN (CORNWALL), ST. PETROC'S; font. *Circa* 1200.

This font is an outstanding example of the Cornish group. Some other fonts of this type are at St. Austell, St. Stephen-in-Brannel, St. Kea, East Newlyn and Roche.

102. STAFFORD, ST. MARY'S; font. *Circa* 1200.

Highly original font supported by lions, whose evil significance is explained by the inscription: DISCRETUS NON ES SI NON FUGIS ECCE LEONES.

103. TUTBURY (STAFFORDSHIRE), PRIORY OF ST. MARY ; detail of west doorway. *Circa* 1180.

The elaborate treatment of the decoration is combined, in this case, with the use of alabaster in one of the orders. The sculpture shows, however, a definite decline in quality.

104. IFFLEY (OXFORDSHIRE), ST. MARY'S; detail of west doorway. *Between* 1175 *and* 1182.

One of the most accomplished doorways with the beak-head ornament as the principal form of decoration. On the label is a chain-motive with the Signs of the Zodiac and the symbols of the Evangelists.

105—107. IFFLEY; details of south doorway.

108. IFFLEY; detail of angle-shaft of chancel.

109. IFFLEY; boss of chancel vault.

110. ELKSTONE (GLOUCESTERSHIRE), ST. JOHN THE EVANGELIST; boss of chancel. *Circa* 1180.

111. CANTERBURY, CATHEDRAL LIBRARY; relief with prophet. *Circa* 1190.

This relief probably decorated the west front of the Almonry Chapel. It is a transitional work, showing a classical style of Byzantine inspiration.

112. BOBBING (KENT), ST. BARTHOLOMEW'S; ? fragment of door-jamb. *Circa* 1200.

The figure of the bishop is inscribed: " SANCTUS MARCIALIS PIUS PATRONUS." He is attended by another figure, probably a disciple. The sculpture which had been re-used as building material, was found in 1863. The style of the carving is related to the previous relief, though it is less accomplished. The subject is puzzling, because St. Marcial of Limoges was not the patron-saint of Bobbing. He was, however, venerated at St. Augustine's Abbey, Canterbury.

113—114. MUCH WENLOCK (SHROPSHIRE), PRIORY OF HOLY TRINITY; reliefs of cloister lavatory. *Circa* 1190.

One relief represents two figures of saints or prophets, the other the *Calling of St. Peter*. The style of the reliefs is related to that of the fonts at Stanton Fitzwarren and Southrop (Figs. 97—98).

115—116. LONDON, VICTORIA AND ALBERT MUSEUM; fragment of statuette from Bridlington Priory, 1170—1180.

The fragment was part of a figure carved in the round and placed in a niche. It shows a style parallel to that of the Copenhagen Psalter (Fig. 117), which was executed in an Augustinian house in Yorkshire about 1170. Bridlington was an Augustinian Priory and the Psalter may have originated there.

117. COPENHAGEN, ROYAL LIBRARY; English Psalter. *Circa* 1170.

The *Visitation* scene.

118—125. YORK, YORKSHIRE MUSEUM; figures from west front of St. Mary's Abbey, York. *Circa* 1210.

The most important group of sculptures in the transitional style in England. They are inspired by the early Gothic works of the Ile-de-France, but modified in their style by the classical element derived from Byzantine sources. Figs. 118—119 show Moses, Fig. 121, a beardless young man, possibly St. John the Evangelist. Another figure, not illustrated here, is St. John the Baptist. The series consists of ten figures. Originally there were probably more and they represented the forerunners of Christ and the Apostles.

126. YORK, YORKSHIRE MUSEUM; voussoir from St. Mary's Abbey, York. *Circa* 1210.

One of the four voussoirs forming the arch of the doorway or doorways, to which the previous figures also belonged. The carving represents *Herod ordering the Massacre of the Innocents* and is placed under two arcades covered by a canopy. It is interesting to compare this voussoir with an illumination in a Psalter from Northern England representing the same subject, where a similar Byzantine influence is apparent (see Fig. 127).

127. OXFORD, BODLEIAN LIBRARY; Psalter (MS. Gough Liturg.). *Circa* 1200.

The Massacre of the Innocents.

128. LINCOLN CATHEDRAL; statue on west front. *Early thirteenth century.*

One of the two statues placed in niches flanking the central doorway. Their heads and hands are modern restorations. They are transitional in style.

129—130. GLASTONBURY ABBEY (SOMERSET); details of north doorway of Lady Chapel. *Circa* 1210.

The Lady Chapel was built after the fire of 1184 and was consecrated in 1186. The two doorways, of which the north was the principal entrance, were carved *in situ* at a later date. The sculptures are already early Gothic, retaining, however, some traces of the classicism of the transitional period. The sculptor of the Glastonbury doorways later worked at Wells Cathedral.

131. DURHAM, ST. MARY-THE-LESS; relief formerly in St. Giles, Durham. *Early thirteenth century.*

The sculpture represents *Christ in Majesty* within a mandorla and surrounded by the symbols of the Evangelists. In this work, the Byzantine element is transformed by the early Gothic stylization. Similar tendencies occur in manuscript paintings such as that shown in the following illustration.

132. LONDON, BRITISH MUSEUM; Psalter from Westminster Abbey (Royal MS. 2A, xxii, f. 14r). *Circa* 1200.

133. BRIDLINGTON (YORKSHIRE), PRIORY OF ST. MARY; label stop of cloister arcade. *Early thirteenth century*.

The chevron arcades and, to a certain extent the foliage, are still Romanesque but the head shows a change of treatment and spirit that announce a new art. The Gothic naturalism took the place of the Romanesque symbolism and love of stylized pattern.

ACKNOWLEDGEMENTS

The author wishes to express his gratitude to all whose who directly or indirectly helped him in writing this essay. He owes a particular debt to Professor T. S. R. Boase, M. Jean Bony, Dr. C. R. Dodwell, Mr. Christopher Hohler, Mr. Peter Lasko, Dr. Hanns Swarzenski and Professor Francis Wormald for their generous advice and help.

He also wishes to thank the following for permission to reproduce photographs : Mrs. Trenchard Cox (Figs. 2 and 98) ; Mr. F. H. Crossley (Figs. 4, 5, 8, 12, 13, 41, 46, 48, 71, 72, 102, 110) ; Mr. F. R. Kersting (Fig. 69), Archives Photographiques (Figs. 33, 95) ; Corpus Christi College, Cambridge (Fig. 68) ; Guildhall Museum (Fig. 27) ; Marburg Institute (Fig. 56) ; National Buildings Record (Figs, 3, 6, 7, 11, 44, 47, 49, 50, 52, 54, 55, 57 59-63, 101, 103, 128) ; Bodleian Library, Oxford (Fig. 127) ; Royal Commission on Historical Monuments (Fig. 32) ; Warburg Institute (Figs. 36, 37, 66, 92-94).

Finally he would like to thank Miss Elizabeth Edmonds for reading the text and proofs and the Photographic Department of the Courtauld Institute for invaluable help.

INDEX

of names and places mentioned in volumes one and two.

(The page references are given in ordinary numerals and the plate references in bold numerals)

1. LONDON, WESTMINSTER ABBEY—capital. *Judgement of Solomon.*
Circa 1140

2. AVINGTON (BERKSHIRE)—font. *Circa* 1140

3. DARENTH (KENT), ST. MARGARET'S—font *Rite of Baptism.*
Circa 1140

4. AVEBURY (WILTSHIRE), ST. JAMES'—font. *Christ tramping
two beasts. Circa* 1140

5. ALPHINGTON (DEVON), ST. MICHAEL'S—font. *Circa* 1140

6. COLESHILL (WARWICKSHIRE), ST. PETER AND ST. PAUL
—font. *Crucifixion. Circa* 1150

7. COLESHILL (WARWICKSHIRE), ST. PETER AND ST. PAUL
—detail of font. *A Saint. Circa* 1150

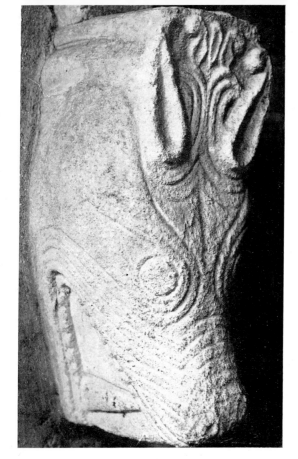

8. DEERHURST (GLOUCESTER-SHIRE), HOLY TRINITY—label stop. *10th century*

9. LONDON, VICTORIA & ALBERT MUSEUM — beak-heads from Reading Abbey. *Circa* 1130

10. OXFORD, ST. EBBE'S—detail of west doorway. *Circa* 1150

11. BARFORD (OXFORDSHIRE), ST. MICHAEL'S—detail of north doorway. *Circa* 1150

12—13. BISHOP'S TEIGNTON (DEVON), ST. JOHN'S—details of west doorway. *Third quarter of the 12th century*

14—15. NORTHAMPTON, ST. PETER'S—capitals. *Circa* 1150

16—17. NORTHAMPTON. ST. PETER'S—capitals. *Circa* 1150

18.   NORTHAMPTON,
ST. PETER'S—tomb-slab.
Circa 1150

19. KILPECK (HEREFORDSHIRE), ST. MARY AND ST. DAVID
—south doorway. *Circa* 1150

20. KILPECK (HEREFORDSHIRE)—detail of
south doorway. *Circa* 1150

21. KILPECK (HERE-
FORDSHIRE)—detail of
chancel arch. *Circa* 1150

—24. KILPECK (HEREFORDSHIRE)—details of south doorway. *Circa* 1150

25. EAR
SLEY (HE
FORDSHI
S T . M A
MAGDALI
—detail of
Circa 1150

26. KILPECK (HEREFORDSHIRE)—corbel.
Circa 1150

27. LONDON, GUILDHA
MUSEUM—Viking comb. 1
century.

CASTLE FROME (HERE-
ORDSHIRE), ST.
ICHAEL'S — detail of font.
ca 1150

29. KILPECK (HEREFORD-
SHIRE)—corbel. *Circa* 1150

30. CASTLE FROME (HEREFORDSHIRE)—detail of font. *Baptism of Christ. Circa* 1150

31. BRINSOP (HEREFORDSHIRE), ST. GEORGE'S—tympanum.
St. George. Circa 1150

32. STRETTON SUGWAS (HEREFORDSHIRE), ST. MARY
MAGDALEN'S—tympanum. *Samson and the lion. Circa* 1150

33. PARTHENAY-LE-VIEUX (DEUX-SEVRES)—west front. *Circa* 1120

34. STOTTESDON (SHROPSHIRE), ST. MARY'S—font. *Circa* 1160

35. CHADDESLEY CORBETT (WORCESTERSHIRE), ST.
CASSIAN'S—font. *Circa* 1160

36. DURHAM CATHEDRAL—cary-
atid from chapter house. *Circa* 1140

37. DURHAM CATHEDRAL—cary-
atid from chapter house. *Circa* 1140

38—39. WINCHESTER CATHEDRAL—font. *Story of St. Nicholas.*
Third quarter of the 12th century

40. SALISBURY MUSEUM—capital from Old Sarum. *Third quarter of the 12th century*

41. ELY CATHEDRAL—tomb-slab. *Third quarter of the 12th century.*

42. SALISBURY MUSEUM — top of gable from Old Sarum. *Circa* 1140

43. SALISBURY MUSEUM — beak-head from Old Sarum. *Circa* 1140

44. LINCOLN CATHEDRAL —detail of central doorway. *Circa* 1145

45. SALISBURY MUSEUM—head from apex of arch from Old Sarum. *Circa* 1140

46. MALMESBURY ABBEY (WILTSHIRE)—head at apex of nave arcade. *Circa* 1160

47. LINCOLN CATHEDRAL—detail of central doorway. *Circa* 1145

48. MALMESBURY ABBEY (WILTSHIRE)—label stop of nave arcade. *Circa* 1160·

49. LINCOLN CATHEDRAL—detail of central doorway. *Circa* 1145.

50. LINCOLN CATHEDRAL—capital of north doorway.

51. SAINT-DENIS CATHEDRAL—capital in narthex. *Between* 1137

detail of column
doorway. *Circa*
1145

53. S A I N T-
DENIS CATH-
EDRAL.—detail
of north door-
way. *Between
1137 and 1140*

54—55. LINCOLN CATHEDRAL—details of central doorway.
Circa 1145

56. SAINT-DENIS CATHEDRAL—detail of south doorway. *Between* 1137 *and* 1140

57. LINCOLN CATHEDRAL—frieze. *Cain and Abel. Circa* 1145

59. LINCOLN CATHEDRAL—frieze. *Noah leaving the Ark. Circa* 1145

58. SAINT-DENIS CATHEDRAL.—detail of north doorway. *Between* 1137 *and* 1140

60. LINCOLN CATHEDRAL—frieze. *Noah building the Ark. Circa* 1145

61. LINCOLN CATHEDRAL—frieze. *Dives and Lazarus. Circa* 1145

62. LINCOLN CATHEDRAL—frieze. ? *Apostles. Circa* 1145

63. LINCOLN CATHEDRAL—frieze. *Doom and Harrowing of Hell.*   *Circa* 1145

64. YORK MINSTER—*Virgin and Child.* ? 1154

BARKING ABBEY
(ESSEX)—detail of Rood.
St. John. Circa 1150

66. WAREHAM (DOR-
SET), ST. MARY'S—detail
of lead font. *Circa* 1150

67. DURHAM CATHEDRAL—relief of original screen. *Between* 1150 *and* 1160

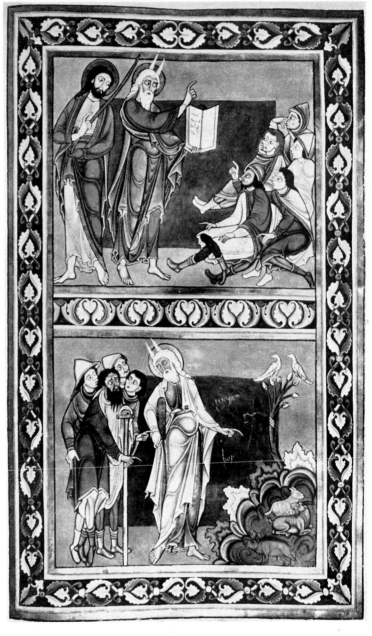

68. CAMBRIDGE, CORPUS CHRISTI COLLEGE—Bible of Bury
St. Edmunds (MS. 2, fol. 94r.) *Before* 1148

69. LENTON (NOTTINGHAMSHIRE), HOLY TRINITY—font.
Third quarter of the 12th century

70a—b. BRIGHTON (SUSSEX), ST. NICHOLAS'—font. *Third quarter of the 12th century*

71. BRIDEKIRK (CUMBERLAND), ST. BRIDGET'S—font. *Third quarter of the 12th century*

72. BRIDEKIRK (CUMBERLAND), ST. BRIDGET'S—font. *Third quarter of the 12th century*

73. SELBY ABBEY (YORKSHIRE), capital of nave. *Circa* 1140

74. BRAYTON (YORKSHIRE), ST. WILFRID'S—capitals of chancel
arch. *Circa* 1150

75—76. BRAYTON (YORKSHIRE)—details of south doorway.
Circa 1150

77—78. YORK MINSTER—capitals of crypt. *Circa* 1160

79—80. YORK, YORKSHIRE MUSEUM—voussoirs of doorway
Circa 1160

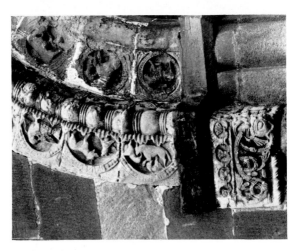

81—82. ALNE (YORKSHIRE). ST. MARY'S—details of south
doorway. *Circa* 1160

83—84. FISHLAKE (YORKSHIRE), ST. CUTHBERT'S—
details of south doorway. 1160—1170

85. ROCHESTER CATHEDRAL—west doorway. *Circa* 1160 *with later insertions*

86. ROCHESTER CATHEDRAL—west doorway. *Circa* 1160 *with later insertions*

87—89. BARFRESTON (KENT), S T MARY'S—details of south doorway. *Circa* 1180

90. BARFRESTON (KENT), ST. MARY'S—details of south doorway.
Circa 1180

91. BARFRESTON (KENT)—capital of north doorway. *Circa* 1180

92. MALMESBURY ABBEY (WILTSHIRE)—tympanum on east wall of porch. 1160—1170

93. MALMESBURY ABBEY (WILTSHIRE)—detail of tympanum
on west wall of porch. 1160—1170

94. MALMESBURY ABBEY (WILTSHIRE)—detail of outer doorway. *Entombment of Christ*. 1160—1170

95. AULNAY-DE-SAINTONGE (CHARENTE-INFERIEURE), ST.
PIERRE—detail of west doorway. *Second quarter of the 12th century*

96.   MALMESBURY ABBEY (WILTSHIRE)—detail of outer doorway.
1160—1170

97. STANTON FITZWARREN (WILTSHIRE), ST. LEONARD'S
—font. *Circa* 1180

98. SOUTHROP (GLOUCESTERSHIRE), ST. PETER'S—font.
Circa 1180

99. SHERNBORNE (NORFOLK), ST. PETER AND ST. PAUL—
font. *Circa* 1170

100.   GREAT KIMBLE (BUCKINGHAMSHIRE), ST. NICHOLAS'
—font. *Circa* 1180

101. BODMIN (CORNWALL), PRIORY OF ST. PETROC—font.
Circa 1200

102. STAFFORD, ST. MARY'S—font. *Circa* 1200

103. TUTBURY (STAFFORDSHIRE), ST. MARY'S—detail of west doorway. *Circa* 1180

104. IFFLEY (OXFORDSHIRE), ST. MARY'S — detail of west doorway. *Between* 1175 *and* 1182

105. IFFLEY (OXFORD-SHIRE)—detail of south door-way. *Between 1175 and 1182*

106—107. IFFLEY (OXFORD-SHIRE)—capitals of south door-way. *Between 1175 and 1182*

108. IFFLEY (OXFORDSHIRE)—detail of angle-shaft of chancel.
Between 1175 *and* 1182

109. IFFLEY (OXFORDSHIRE)—boss of chancel vault

110. ELKSTONE (GLOUCESTERSHIRE), ST. JOHN THE
EVANGELIST—boss of chancel vault. *Circa* 1180

111. CANTERBURY, CATHEDRAL LIBRARY—relief with prophet.
Circa 1190

112. BOBBING (KENT), ST. BARTHOLOMEW'S—? fragment of
door-jamb. *St. Martial. Circa* 1200

113. MUCH WENLOCK PRIORY (SHROPSHIRE)—relief of
cloister lavatory. *Circa* 1190

114. MUCH WENLOCK PRIORY (SHROPSHIRE)—relief of cloister lavatory. *Circa* 1190

115—116. LONDON, VICTORIA AND ALBERT MUSEUM—statuette from Bridlington Priory. 1170—1180

117. COPENHAGEN, ROYAL LIBRARY—English Psalter. *Circa* 1170

118—119. YORK, YORKSHIRE MUSEUM—figure of Moses from Mary's Abbey, York. *Circa* 1210

120—121. YORK, YORKSHIRE MUSEUM—figures from St. Mary's Abbey, York. *Circa* 1210

122—123.   YORK, YORKSHIRE MUSEUM—
figure from St. Mary's Abbey, York. *Circa* 1210

124—125. YORK, YORKSHIRE MUSEUM—details of figures from St. Mary's Abbey, York. *Circa* 1210

126. YORK, YORKSHIRE MUSEUM—voussoir from
St. Mary's Abbey. *Massacre of Innocents. Circa* 1210

127. OXFORD.   BODLEIAN   LIBRARY—Psalter.
Massacre of Innocents. Circa 1200

128. LINCOLN CATHEDRAL—statue on west front (head modern).
Early 13th century

131. DURHAM, ST. MARY-THE-LESS—relief of *Majesty*, formerly in St. Giles's. *Early 13th century*

132. LONDON, BRITISH MUSEUM—Psalter from Westminster Abbey. *Circa* 1200

133. BRIDLINGTON PRIORY (YORKSHIRE)—cloister arcade.
Early 13th century